The Knowledge of the Truth - Two Doctrines

European University Studies

Europäische Hochschulschriften
Publications Universitaires Européennes

Series XXIII
Theology

Reihe XXIII   Série XXIII
Theologie
Théologie

Bd./Vol. 194

PETER LANG
Frankfurt am Main · Bern

Jesse Sell

The Knowledge of the Truth – Two Doctrines

The Book of Thomas the Contender (CG II,7) and the False Teachers in the Pastoral Epistles

PETER LANG
Frankfurt am Main · Bern

CIP-Kurztitelaufnahme der Deutschen Bibliothek

Sell, Jesse:

The knowledge of the truth - two doctrines :
the book of Thomas the Contender (CG II,7) and the
false teachers in the Pastoral Epistles / Jesse
Sell. - Frankfurt am Main ; Bern : Lang, 1982.
  (European university studies : Ser. 23, Theology ;
  Bd. 194)
  ISBN 3-8204-7224-X
NE: Europäische Hochschulschriften / 23

BS
2735.5
.S4
1982

ISSN 0721-3409
ISBN 3-8204-7224-X
©Verlag Peter Lang GmbH, Frankfurt am Main 1982
Alle Rechte vorbehalten.
Nachdruck oder Vervielfältigung, auch auszugsweise, in allen Formen
wie Mikrofilm, Xerographie, Mikrofiche, Mikrocard, Offset verboten.

Druck und Bindung: fotokop wilhelm weihert KG, darmstadt

For Kathryn

TABLE OF CONTENTS

INTRODUCTION 1

CHAPTER

   I   FORMAL DEFINITION OF THE TERMS 3

  II   "CONTENT DEFINITIONS" OF THE TERMS 9

 III   POSSIBLE HISTORICAL PARALLELS
       IN GREEK TEXTS 31

  IV   POSSIBLE PARALLELS IN
       NAG HAMMADI TEXTS 45

   V   THE DOCTRINE OF THOMAS THE CONTENDER
       AND THE "FALSE TEACHINGS" 69

  VI   SUMMARY AND CONCLUSIONS:
       THE POSSIBLE HISTORICAL IMPLICATIONS 79

NOTES 83

BIBLIOGRAPHY 105

INTRODUCTION

The exact nature of the struggle against false teaching ("heresy" or "heresies") reflected in the Pastoral Epistles has long puzzled New Testament scholarship. It has often been suggested, of course, that it may have involved conflict with some sort of "Gnosticism," or "gnosticizing" party (parties). The vast body of new material from primary "Gnostic" sources available in the Nag Hammadi Coptic corpus has not, however, yet been applied to this problem. I would suggest that evidence from a short and little-discussed tractate in that corpus, The Book of Thomas the Contender (CG II,7),(1) allows the Pastorals' struggle against false teaching to be viewed from an historical perspective not before available to New Testament scholarship. The purpose of this study will be to outline that evidence and then to propose a specific two-part hypothesis related to that struggle.

The general character of Thom. Cont. may be depicted quite succinctly. It consists of two basic sections: 1) a dialogue between "the Savior," an obvious representation of the risen Jesus Christ, and his brother Thomas (138,4-142,26a); 2) a monologue by "the Savior" (142,26b-146,16) which, Turner has suggested, may represent a late stage of the traditions of the "sayings of Jesus."(2) The two sections differ, not only in literary form, but in other significant ways. It seems best, therefore, to accept -- at least as a working hypothesis -- Turner's suggestion that the two sections represent separate traditions which have been redacted to form the present text.(3)

The text is, at least in the broad sense of the term, "gnostic." "The Savior" brings (sometimes rather esoteric) revelations to Thomas, knowledge of which alone makes salvation possible. An extreme, especially anti-sexual, asceticism is by far the most prominent feature of the entire tractate. It must also be emphasized that, no matter how aberrant its teachings appear, the text of Thom. Cont. was composed by those who considered themselves and their doctrine "Christian." The lost Greek Vorlage (Vorlagen) of the extant Coptic version should, probably, best be dated in the early third century.(4)

The phrase "ⲡⲥⲟⲟⲩⲛ̄ⲛ̄ⲧⲙⲏⲉ" ("the knowledge of the truth") appears in Thom. Cont. (at 138,13) in the introductory portion of the dialogue section. Nearly seventy years ago Dibelius argued that "ἐπίγνωσις ἀληθείας" was used as an emphatic technical term in the Pastorals,(5) a technical term best seen as such in polemic passages against false teaching ("heresy").(6) The remarkable relationship I find between that Pastoral technical term and, the -- I am convinced -- equally emphatic Coptic technical term "ⲡⲥⲟⲟⲩⲛ̄ⲛ̄ⲧⲙⲏⲉ," is the foundation for this entire study. The relationship between those two technical terms for "the knowledge of the truth" provides the key to that new evidence I believe

Thom. Cont. provides allowing the Pastorals' struggle against false teaching to be viewed from an historical perspective not previously available.

Chapter I
FORMAL DEFINITION OF THE TERMS

I shall briefly review Dibelius's analysis of the technical term "ἐπίγνωσις ἀληθείας," and then indicate an additional facet of the term's meaning I find implicit in his work, in order to present my own purely formally-defined statement of the technical meaning of that term. "ἐπίγνωσις ἀληθείας" appears at 1 Tim. 2:4; 2 Tim. 2:25, 3:7; Tit. 1:1. Since "γνῶσις" and "ἐπίγνωσις" appear basically interchangeable in the Bible,(1) Dibelius took special note of the absolutely unvarying and stereotyped form of that (technical) term in the Pastorals.(2) He considered the possibility that the generally anti-Gnostic character of those epistles might account for the consistent usage of "ἐπίγνωσις" (rather than "γνῶσις") in the phrase in question.(3) He, however, preferred to attribute the phenomenon to a "bereits vorhandenen Sprachgebrauch"(4) -- also probably reflected in the equally technical term "τὴν ἐπίγνωσιν τῆς ἀληθείας" appearing at Heb. 10:26.

The meaning of this technical term in the Pastorals was, admittedly, affected by their "rationalistic" tenor.(5) Since, however, the term was used as a "paraphrase" for "Christsein,"(6) "everything involved in 'being Christian'[my language]," it must also reflect -- in its full meaning -- the fact that, for those epistles: "Nur freilich ist Christentum nicht blosses Verständnis der Lehre, sondern - das bezeugt jedes Kapitel der...Briefe - Lehre und Leben verbunden."(7) Dibelius's most explicit 1914 definition of the term "ἐπίγνωσις ἀληθείας" as a representation of "Christsein" was, therefore: "...die christliche Erkenntnis, die aus der rechten Lehre stammt und sich im Leben auswirkt."(8) It thus represented (my paraphrase): "the (not merely 'intellectual') understanding which arises from (the apprehending of) the correct Christian doctrine, an understanding which necessarily expresses itself in one's way of life."

Dibelius also intimated, however, an additional important facet of that term's technical meaning, one I find applicable to all the Pastoral usages (and to the meaning of the similar phrase at Heb. 10:26). He suggested: "Können σωθῆναι...und εἰς ἐπίγνωσιν ἀληθείας ἐλθεῖν 1. Tim 2, 4, parallel stehen...."(9) I would even take "καί" in "σωθῆναι καὶ εἰς ἐπίγνωσιν ἀληθείας ἐλθεῖν" (1 Tim. 2:4) as a "καί explicative" and translate: "to be saved, that is, to come to the knowledge of the truth."(10) In his own commentary on the Pastorals Dibelius states, moreover, that at 2 Tim. 2:25 and 3:7 "ἐπίγνωσις ἀληθείας": "...zur Umschreibung des vollen Heilsstandes dient."(11)

Dibelius's remarks about these three passages obviously imply that the technical meaning of the term is also (my language): "always intimately related to 'being saved,' to the whole matter of 'soteriology'" -- a matter which is most surely part of "Christsein" ("everything involved in 'being Christian'"). Exegesis of the four Pastoral passages, and of Heb. 10:26, supports the addition of this dimension to the meaning of the technical term in question. Here, for the sake of brevity, I shall cite only the evidence on this facet of the term's meaning yielded by exegesis of 2 Tim. 2:25-26 and 1 Tim. 2:3-4.(12)

"ἐπίγνωσις ἀληθείας" appears at 2 Tim. 2:25-26 in a polemic context, controversy with those who do not hold "correct" Christian doctrine. These opponents are, however, to be treated gently because: "God may perhaps grant that they will repent and come to know the truth ["δῴη αὐτοῖς ὁ θεὸς μετάνοιαν εἰς ἐπίγνωσιν ἀληθείας"], and they may escape from the snare of the devil...." (13) "God," who may grant this "repentance into the knowledge of the truth,"(14) is the same "God" called (at 1 Tim. 2:3b-4): "God our Savior ["τοῦ σωτῆρος ἡμῶν θεοῦ"], who desires all men to be saved, that is ["καὶ"], to come to the knowledge of the truth."(15) The result of this "repentance into the knowledge of the truth" is: "...escape from the snare of the devil...." (2 Tim. 2:26) This repentance "εἰς ἐπίγνωσιν ἀληθείας" is thus granted by the God: who is "our Savior"; who "desires all men to be saved...." This repentance "εἰς ἐπίγνωσιν ἀληθείας" also allows: "...escape from the snare of the devil...." Surely this passage clearly associates "being saved" with the meaning of the phrase "ἐπίγνωσις ἀληθείας" as a technical term.(16)

The "soteriological" aspect of the technical meaning of the term "ἐπίγνωσις ἀληθείας" in the other passage (1 Tim. 2:3-4) should be clear just from what has already been said. The "parallel" infinitives, "σωθῆναι," and "(εἰς ἐπίγνωσιν ἀληθείας) ἐλθεῖν," are both objects of the desire of the God who is specifically identified as "our Savior"; and who, according to the relative clause: "...desires all men to be saved, that is, to come to the knowledge of the truth." Clearly there is a "functional" synonymity in this passage between "to be saved" and "to come to the knowledge of the truth." "Being saved" is certainly clearly associated with the meaning of "ἐπίγνωσις ἀληθείας" at 1 Tim. 2:4.

I may, therefore, offer this purely formally-defined statement of the full technical meaning of the term "ἐπίγνωσις ἀληθείας" in the Pastoral Epistles. That term represents an "understanding" which: a) is of "correct Christian doctrine"; b) "necessarily expresses itself in one's way of life"; c) is then "intimately related to 'being saved,' to the whole matter of 'soteriology.'" The term is also, therefore, certainly a quite legitimate representation of "Christsein" -- "everything involved in 'being Christian.'"(17)

I shall now demonstrate, as briefly as possible, the striking phenomenon crucial to all my argument to follow. It can clearly be shown that when "ⲡⲥⲟⲟⲩⲛ︦ⲧⲙⲏⲉ" in Thom. Cont. is defined, from its context (CG II: 138,7-21) -- <u>purely formally</u> without regard to <u>any</u> "content definition" -- the <u>purely formal</u> definition of "ἐπίγνωσις ἀληθείας" just offered also fits that Coptic phrase perfectly! These two terms for "the knowledge of the truth" are synonymous as <u>purely formally-defined</u> technical terms!

The establishment of that purely formal technical definition of "ⲡⲥⲟⲟⲩⲛⲛ̄ⲧⲙⲏⲉ" rests upon three indisputable presuppositions, two of which have already been pointed out. 1) The revealer figure in <u>Thom. Cont.</u> is clearly meant to represent the "Jesus Christ" of the canonical New Testament. 2) The epithets normally used to characterize that figure are, however: "the Savior (σωτήρ)"; "Savior (σωτήρ)." 3) Those responsible for the composition of the <u>Vorlage</u> of <u>Thom. Cont.</u> considered themselves and their doctrine "Christian."

It may be shown quite easily, from the logic of the <u>immediate context</u> in which "ⲡⲥⲟⲟⲩⲛⲛ̄ⲧⲙⲏⲉ" appears, that two facets of the purely formal definition of that Coptic term are synonymous with two of the facets of the purely formal definition of the Greek term "ἐπίγνωσις ἀληθείας." "The Savior" tells Thomas: "You have already understood me...."(18) Then, in a nominal sentence of self-predication, he <u>identifies</u> "me": "I am the knowledge of the truth ["ⲁⲛⲟⲕ ⲡⲉ ⲡⲥⲟⲟⲩⲛ ⲛ̄ⲧⲙⲏⲉ"]." (138,13b) "I," the "me" whom Thomas has understood, is, therefore, logically interchangeable with "ⲡⲥⲟⲟⲩⲛ ⲛ̄ⲧⲙⲏⲉ." An "understanding" of "ⲡⲥⲟⲟⲩⲛ ⲛ̄ⲧⲙⲏⲉ" thus actually represents an "understanding" of the "me" ("I") who <u>is</u> "the Savior"; who also represents "Jesus Christ." To have an "understanding" of "ⲡⲥⲟⲟⲩⲛ ⲛ̄ⲧⲙⲏⲉ," therefore, is to have an "understanding" of "Jesus Christ" -- certainly the Ultimate Subject of "correct Christian doctrine." It is also, therefore, to have an "understanding" of "the Savior," an "understanding" which is then quite obviously "intimately related to 'being saved,' to the whole matter of 'soteriology.'"

A much more complex argument is required to show that the third facet of the formal definition of "ἐπίγνωσις ἀληθείας" is also formally represented by "ⲡⲥⲟⲟⲩⲛⲛ̄ⲧⲙⲏⲉ." That argument rests upon the subtle -- but sure -- implications of the logical connection between the sections into which CG II: 138,7-21 may be divided. The more complex analysis required to demonstrate that an "understanding" of "ⲡⲥⲟⲟⲩⲛⲛ̄ⲧⲙⲏⲉ" "necessarily expresses itself in one's way of life" should also reinforce my arguments regarding the two other facets of the term's formal definition. It should indicate that they are not based just upon the formal interchangeability of "I," "me," and "ⲡⲥⲟⲟⲩⲛⲛ̄ⲧⲙⲏⲉ." That is, my argument directed toward the <u>third</u> facet of the formally-defined meaning of "ⲡⲥⲟⲟⲩⲛⲛ̄ⲧⲙⲏⲉ," an argument based entirely upon the complex logical relationship between the parts into which 138,7-21 may be divided, partly consists of an argument which <u>also</u> shows that "ⲡⲥⲟⲟⲩⲛⲛ̄ⲧⲙⲏⲉ" represents an "understanding" of "correct Christian doctrine."(19)

The last eight parts (of the twelve) into which my translation divides 138,7-21 must be inserted here to preface those arguments. I would translate, and divide the translation of, CG II: 138,12b-21a in this manner.

5) "I know that you have understood"(138,12b); 6) "because (γάρ) you have already understood me [that]: 'I am the knowledge of the truth.'" (138,12b-13); 7) "While now (ὡς) you are walking with me, even though (κἄν) you are ignorant,"(138,14); 8) "you have already known"(138,15a); 9) "and you will be called: 'the one who knows himself.'"(138,15b-16a); 10) "For (γάρ) the one who has not known himself has not known anything; but (δέ) the one who has known himself also has already grasped knowledge of the Depth (βάθος) of the All."(138,16b-18); 11) "On account of this you are my brother, Thomas."(138,19a); 12) "You have seen that which is hidden from [other] men, that is, that which they stumble on -- they not knowing [it]."(138,19b-21a)

My argument proceeds according to these logical steps. A) It seems, according to "part 7," that Thomas is not yet aware of "the truth." He is called "ignorant." B) Yet, it is then said ("part 8") that: "You [Thomas] have already known...."(20) C) The only possible knowledge Thomas might have already attained would be of "me." "You have already understood me...." ("part 6") That is, he has already understood "ⲡⲥⲟⲟⲩⲛⲛ̅ⲧⲙⲏⲉ."

D) It is clear from "parts 8-9" that this knowledge Thomas has already attained -- his knowledge of "ⲡⲥⲟⲟⲩⲛⲛ̅ⲧⲙⲏⲉ" -- will now result in Thomas's coming to "know himself." "You have already known and [, therefore,] you will be called: 'the one who knows himself.'" E) According to "part 10": "One who has not known himself has not known anything; but (δέ) the one who has known himself [because he has known "ⲡⲥⲟⲟⲩⲛⲛ̅ⲧⲙⲏⲉ"] also has already grasped knowledge of the Depth (βάθος) of the All." F) If one who has not known himself has known nothing, the contrary state of the one who does know himself (because he has known "ⲡⲥⲟⲟⲩⲛ ⲛ̅ⲧⲙⲏⲉ") would seem clearly that of one who knows "everything (of import)." The impressive language used to describe what this self-knower also knows -- "knowledge of the Depth (βάθος) of the All ["ⲡⲧⲏⲣϥ"] -- (21) certainly supports such an interpretation. G) The knowledge described by that "impressive language," which is the possession of one in a quite different state from that of knowing nothing, may thus be quite reasonably taken as representing "everything [important about crucial matters]" -- in a "Christian" text such as Thom. Cont.: "correct Christian doctrine"! That knowledge, in context, is clearly also an "understanding" only possible because one has "already known ["understood"] me" -- as "ⲡⲥⲟⲟⲩⲛⲛ̅ⲧⲙⲏⲉ."

This argument about "correct Christian doctrine," which had already been shown to represent a facet of the "understanding" of "ⲡⲥⲟⲟⲩⲛⲛ̅ⲧⲙⲏⲉ," has been presented here in order to show how certainly it is also indicated in "parts 11-12" that this "understanding" is one which "necessarily expresses itself in one's way of life." A) "On account of this" -- the "understanding" of "correct Christian doctrine" ("part 10") ultimately derived from having "understood" "me" as "ⲡⲥⲟⲟⲩⲛⲛ̄ⲧⲙⲏⲉ": "You are my brother, Thomas. You have seen that which is hidden from [other] men." "That which is hidden from [other] men" is obviously only a different way of describing Thomas's "understanding" (already emphatically stated in "part 6") of "correct Christian doctrine" arising directly from "understanding" "ⲡⲥⲟⲟⲩⲛⲛ̄ⲧⲙⲏⲉ." B) <u>Crucially</u>, however, the latter portion of "part 12" finally makes it clear that this "understanding" of "correct Christian doctrine" -- as it is described in "part 10" -- is <u>also</u> an "understanding" which: "necessarily expresses itself in one's way of life." Those to whom what Thomas <u>has</u> "seen" ("understood") -- in "part 10" -- is "hidden," "<u>stumble</u>"; they stumble <u>precisely because</u> they have <u>not</u> "seen," or "understood," what Thomas <u>has</u> "seen" and "understood." "You have seen that which is hidden from [other] men, that is, <u>that which they stumble on</u> -- they <u>not</u> knowing [it]." Obviously, therefore, Thomas will <u>not stumble</u>. He has "seen," or "understood," what causes "stumbling" for those who do <u>not</u> know ("understand") it. What Thomas has "seen" ("understood"), his already-attained "understanding" of "ⲡⲥⲟⲟⲩⲛⲛ̄ⲧⲙⲏⲉ," <u>will</u>, therefore, express "itself in...[his] way of life."(22)

An "understanding" of "ⲡⲥⲟⲟⲩⲛⲛ̄ⲧⲙⲏⲉ" represents, therefore, an "understanding" which, strictly formally-defined, also represents the third purely formally-defined facet of the technical meaning of "ἐπίγνωσις ἀληθείας." The two terms are thus <u>formally</u> totally synonymous representations of an "understanding" which: a) is of "correct Christian doctrine"; b) "necessarily expresses itself in one's way of life"; c) is then "intimately related to 'being saved,' to the whole matter of 'soteriology.'" The two phrases, formally, also thus represent "Christsein" -- "everything involved in 'being Christian'"!

Chapter II
"CONTENT DEFINITIONS" OF THE TERMS

The result is striking, however, when one compares the "content" definitions" of these two formally synonymous technical terms. Those "content definitions" will be established from the "basic teaching" of "section A" of <u>Thom. Cont.</u>(1) and the "basic teaching" of the Pastorals.

What, according to the teaching of "section A" of <u>Thom. Cont.</u>, actually comprises "correct Christian doctrine"? <u>Its first and most important component is a <u>certain type</u> of "self-knowledge," what Turner calls: "truth about existence in the body."(2) In the words of "the Savior," one must know: "...who you are and how you exist, or (ἤ) in what manner you will exist."(3) What, according to "the Savior," is the proper answer to those questions? "Oh (ὦ) bitterness of the fire that burns in the bodies (σῶμα) of men...making their minds drunk and their souls (ψυχή) deranged...."(4) "For (γάρ) that which guides them, the fire... will blind them with insatiable lust (ἐπιθυμία)....And like a bit (χαλινός) in the mouth it leads them according to its own desire. It fettered them with its chains (ἅλυσις)...in the bitterness of the bond of lust (ἐπιθυμία) for these visible things that will decay and change...."(5) The first element of that "self-knowledge" in question is, therefore, the knowledge that one is <u>now</u> driven and enslaved by bodily desire. That bondage, moreover, links one's <u>future</u> with that of "these visible things that will decay...."

One's state in the body is also described in terms of man's essential likeness to all the other "beasts" in the world. "Does it (the body) not (μήτι) derive from intercourse (συνουσία) like that (body) of the beasts? If it too derives from it (intercourse)...will it (the body) beget anything different (διαφορά) from them (beasts)?"(6) This essentially "bestial" nature, so intimately related to "intercourse," again reflects one's bondage to worldly desire (lust). The <u>present</u> state, described as "bestial," <u>also</u> determines one's <u>future</u>. "Bodies (σῶμα) that are visible eat of creatures similar to them; so, therefore, the bodies (σῶμα) change. But (δέ) that which changes will be destroyed and perish, and has no hope (ἐλπίς) of life from now on, for (γάρ) that body is bestial. So just as the body (σῶμα) of the beasts perishes, so...will these bodies (πλάσμα) perish."(7)

The first component, therefore, of the actual "content" of the "Christian doctrine" represented by "ⲡⲥⲟⲟⲩⲛ︦ⲧ︦ⲙⲏⲉ" -- according to the "basic teaching" of "section A" of <u>Thom. Cont.</u> -- is the self-knowledge that one is driven by bodily desire (lust), just as the other "beasts," and is bound to perish. This self-knowledge can be salutary though -- if it leads to ascetic renunciation of the body, and of all one's worldly desires. "The Savior" thus declares: "O (ὦ) blessed (μακάριος) Thomas, this... light shone for your sakes...that you might come forth; and (δέ) whenever (ὅταν)...the elect abandon bestiality...this light will withdraw (ἀναχωρεῖν)...."(8) The specific injunction of "the Savior" is: "'Everyone who seeks the truth...will make himself wings so as to fly, fleeing the lust (ἐπιθυμία) that scorches the spirits (πνεῦμα) of men.'"(9) This "self-knowledge," the self-knowledge that one is a (bestial) creature driven by desire (lust) and bound to perish unless all one's worldly attachments are denied -- an entirely ascetically oriented point -- is the most clearly defined point of the "content" of the "Christian doctrine" of "section A" of Thom. Cont.!(10)

The second element in the "content" of the "correct Christian doctrine" described by "ⲡⲥⲟⲟⲩⲛ̄ⲛ̄ⲧⲙⲏⲉ" is depicted in the phrase at 138,18b: "knowledge of the Depth (βάθος) of the All." While that "knowledge" is intimately linked to the "self-knowledge" already discussed, it also represents at least one example of the "esoteric doctrines...intended only for the perfect" Martin Krause finds characteristic of Thom. Cont.(11) Such an interpretation of the phrase is in accord with Turner's basic analysis of its meaning. "βάθος is a term often applied to recondite or advanced knowledge while 'the All' generally refers to the Pleroma, to the universe and its structure. Thus something like the knowledge of inner meaning of the universe becomes the possession of those who know themselves."(12) The language of 138,17-18 clearly indicates that the "esoteric," cosmological knowledge indicated by that phrase is meant to represent something additional to the "self-knowledge" discussed. "But (δέ) the one who has known himself also has already grasped knowledge of the Depth (βάθος) of the All."(13)

The third and final aspect of the "content" of the "Christian doctrine" found in "section A" of Thom. Cont. consists of the teaching, that while there is one portion of mankind for whom salvation is possible, there is yet another portion whom "the Savior" himself does not even desire saved. Krause has argued that Thom. Cont. contains, basically, the fully developed (classical) Gnostic doctrine of the division of humanity (by nature) into three distinct classes: the "pneumatics"; the "psychics"; the "hylics."(14) There is at least one clear reference (in a passage already quoted in a different context) to "the elect," those able to act upon the teachings of "the Savior" and thus renounce all bodily desires, those who can therefore be saved. "Whenever (ὅταν) all the elect["ⲥⲱⲧⲡ`"]abandon bestiality, then (τότε) this light will withdraw (ἀναχωρεῖν)...."(15) I find it quite difficult, however, to see clear, unequivocal and specific references to three groups (with destinies fixed from the beginning) in Thom. Cont. Nevertheless, the only possible interpretation of 141,19-27a also requires one to admit that it contains an emphatic statement by "the Savior" that it is not right for a second "class" of men -- apparently most men -- to even have the opportunity to come to saving knowledge.

In that section, after Thomas has received important elements of "the Savior"'s revelation, he asks him: "'What have we to say in the face of these [revealed] things, or (ἤ) what shall we say to blind men, or (ἤ) what teaching should we express to these miserable (ταλαίπωρος) mortals...."(16)   The reply by "the Savior" is striking: "'Truly, as for those, do not esteem (sg) them as men, but regard (sg) them [as (ὡς)] beasts...."(17)   This response must mean that "the Savior" rejects the legitimacy of the salvation of these "blind men."   In light of that response (141, 25b-27a) to Thomas's questions at 141,18-25a, I must challenge Turner's view that those questions seem to represent a reference to preaching to "the elect."(18)   In Turner's own words: "The Savior responds to Thomas' series of questions [at 141,18-25a] with a bitter condemnation of those...unaware of the plight of embodiment."(19)

The third, and final, discernible aspect of the "content" of the "correct Christian doctrine" of "section A" of Thom. Cont., the "understanding" of which represents an important facet of the technical meaning of "ⲡⲥⲟⲟⲩⲛ̄ⲛ̄ⲧⲙⲏⲉ," thus consists of the view that salvation is possible for some "elect" ones (139,28-29); but is not even desirable for other men (141,19-27a).   This last aspect of this facet of the "Christian doctrine" of "section A" of Thom. Cont. will be especially relevant to the discussion of the possible relationship between the "Christianity" presented in that part of Thom. Cont. and that represented by the Pastoral Epistles.

The "content" of the "correct Christian doctrine" to be derived from the "basic teaching" of the Pastoral Epistles is, to say the least, radically different from that derivable from "section A" of Thom. Cont.   The Pastorals' "doctrine" may be described by use of four categories, three of which represent basic and standard categories of Christian dogmatics: 1)"Christology"; 2) "theology" (in the strict sense of that term)(20) ; 3)"pneumatology," the doctrine of the Holy Spirit.   The fourth category is what I shall refer to as: "a doctrine of (about) doctrine." In discussing the first three categories, since this monograph most certainly is not intended to be a "commentary" on the Pastorals, I shall note only the basic aspects of those doctrinal points especially relevant to the comparison of the "Christianity" of the Pastorals and that of "section A" of Thom. Cont.

A relevant aspect of the Christology of the Pastorals appears reflected in the fact that by far the most commonly used term for "Jesus Christ" is "Lord (κύριος)."(21)   On the other hand, "Savior (σωτήρ)"(22) is used only three times of "Jesus Christ" (23) ; but six times of "God the Father."   The Pastorals thus use that term primarily to refer to "God the Father," and only secondarily of "Jesus Christ."   In the Christology of the Pastorals, therefore, "Jesus Christ" is not primarily viewed as "the Savior"; but rather he acts as "Savior" (basically) in the context of his service to "the Savior," "God the Father."   This "subordination" is also reflected in the fact that, while "Lord" is used almost exclusively of "Jesus Christ," the one certain usage of "κύριος" referring to his Father (1 Tim. 6:15) indicates that while "Jesus Christ" may be "the Lord," his Father is "Lord of lords."

In "section A" (or "B") of Thom. Cont., however, "the Savior" is the Revealer who represents "Jesus Christ." "Section A" contains no reference whatsoever to any "God the Father" of "the Savior." In short, in contrast to "section A" of Thom. Cont. where the "Jesus Christ" figure is "the Savior," the Pastorals' Christology basically represents "Jesus Christ" as "Savior" in his role as "agent" of the Ultimate Source of salvation, "the Savior," God his Father!

I cite only one other facet of the Christology of the Pastorals which strikingly differentiates their "Christian doctrine" from that of "section A" of Thom. Cont. They affirm the incarnation of Jesus Christ: Jesus Christ "in the flesh" (1 Tim. 3:16); "the man Christ Jesus" (1 Tim. 2:5). Turner's discussion of the doctrine of Thom. Cont. specifically notes that there is: "...no mention of Christ's life or of his incarnation...."(24) "Jesus Christ" (presumably in his post-resurrection state) is really only significant in Thom. Cont. because of the revelations conveyed just prior to his reascent to the world of light.

The first basic point of the Pastorals' theology, one especially relevant to its relationship to the "Christian doctrine" found in "section A" of Thom. Cont., has already been intimated in the discussion of "Christology." The Pastorals emphatically assert the total sovereignty of the one High God -- not even mentioned in "section A" of Thom. Cont.! The most emphatic statement of that sovereignty is found at 1 Tim. 6:15, where God the Father is proclaimed as: "the blessed and only Sovereign, the King of kings and Lord of lords...." The "Christological" assertion already stated, that Jesus Christ is viewed as "Savior" primarily in his role as the "agent" of "God the Father," may be viewed as a part of this same "theological" posture.

The importance of "theology" (in the strict sense of the term) to the "Christian doctrine" of the Pastorals manifests itself in many ways. For example, the multiplicity of epithets used of "God the Father" seems to demonstrate a desire to "describe" this Central Figure of the Pastorals' Christianity as fully as possible. He is "described" -- to cite only three of the many relevant passages -- as: "the living God"(25) ; the one "who alone has immortality"(26) ; the one "who never lies."(27) Yet, despite this apparent desire to attempt to "describe" "God the Father," the Pastorals nevertheless stress his utter transcendence as one who: "dwells in unapproachable light, whom no man has ever seen or can see."(28) Simultaneously, however, the ultimate New Testament paradox -- unmentioned anywhere in Thom. Cont. -- is maintained by the Pastorals. This one and sovereign

God, ultimately transcendent: "was manifested in the flesh...."
(29)

The Pastorals' theology, moreover, unequivocally and "literally" asserts "monotheism." "For there is one God...."(30) While a "given" of New Testament belief, the literal assertion of monotheism is especially relevant to this discussion because, in Turner's words: "It appears that we do have a <u>hierarchy of divine beings or hypostases</u>, <u>at least in section A of Thomas the Contender</u>...."(31)

This discussion of various aspects of the Pastorals' theology must not be allowed, however, to obscure the one basic and <u>fundamental</u> point of differentiation established by "theology" between the Christianity of the Pastorals and the "Christianity" of <u>Thom. Cont.</u> The "content" of the Pastorals' "correct Christian doctrine" is basically <u>theologically oriented</u>! While "section A" of <u>Thom. Cont.</u> may presuppose a "hierarchy of divine beings," it contains no reference whatsoever to any one High Supreme God with whom "the Savior" has a relationship! The only (probably) direct "theological" statement in the entire tractate is to be found at 145,13-14 -- in "section B": "You will receive rest (ἀνάπαυσις) [sic] from the Good One (ἀγαθός), and you will reign with the King...."(32) It is not even certain that there the <u>same one</u> High God is characterized by the two epithets: "the Good One"; "the King." "In the phrase: 'you will receive rest from the Good One and you will reign with the King,' 'Good One' and 'King' <u>probably</u> designate the same being, God."(33)

The central role "theology" per se occupies in the "Christian doctrine" of the Pastorals sharply differentiates that doctrine -- to say the least -- from the "Christian doctrine" found in "section A" of <u>Thom. Cont.</u>!

"Pneumatology," "the doctrine of the Holy Spirit," is the final "standard" category of Christian dogmatics relevant to this discussion. Its role in defining the overall "content" of the Pastorals' "Christian doctrine" is <u>far</u> less significant than that played by either "Christology" or "theology." Nevertheless, the "Holy Spirit" -- never mentioned or even indirectly alluded to in <u>Thom. Cont.</u> -- does appear as a subject of discussion in the Pastorals.

At Tit. 3:5-7 the reference to the Holy Spirit appears in a basically "soteriological" and "Christological" context: "He saved us...in virtue of his own mercy, by the washing of regeneration and renewal in the Holy Spirit, which he poured out...through Jesus Christ our Savior, so that we might be justified by his grace and become heirs in hope of eternal life." Full exegesis of this complex passage is not required here. Simply the fact that the Pastorals speak of the Holy Spirit -- unmentioned in <u>Thom. Cont.</u> -- in such an important context sharply differentiates the "content" of their "Christian doctrine" from that of "section A" of Thom. Cont. The language at 2 Tim. 1:14 demonstrates the same point: "Guard the truth that has been entrusted to you, by the Holy Spirit who dwells within us." In the Pastorals the Holy Spirit is important. It is the agent of conveying "the truth"; it dwells within the Christian community.

The implications, for this study, of these first three aspects of the "content" of "correct Christian doctrine" in the Pastoral Epistles may be outlined quite clearly. 1) The "Christian doctrine" of Thom. Cont. does not contain any real "Christology" or "theology." Those categories, as Turner unintentionally indicates in his attempted description of the tractate's "theology" and "Christology," are not -- taken in the normal sense of the terms -- at all useful in describing the doctrine of Thom. Cont. His discussion of the text's "theology" deals almost exclusively with the extent to which Thom. Cont. reflects: a)"'The cardinal thought of gnostic theology...the radical dualism that governs the relation of God and the world....'";(34) b)the typical Gnostic "hierarchy of divine beings."(35) As for "Christology," Turner states: "Christology is [only] an issue...because the revealer figure...is twice called 'Jesus,' and sustains relationships with the Christ of the New Testament...." (36) The fact that these two categories, so central to the Pastorals' "Christian doctrine," are basically irrelevant to the "Christian doctrine" of Thom. Cont. could not, thus, be shown more clearly than by Turner's attempt to describe that text's "theology" and "Christology." 2) Since there is absolutely no reference in Thom. Cont. to the "Holy Spirit," to "pneumatology," the first three categories used to describe the "content" of the "Christian doctrine" taught by the Pastorals are, therefore, not at all relevant or useful in describing the version of "Christian doctrine" found in "section A" of Thom. Cont.!

The final, and quite important, category used to describe the "content" of the "Christian doctrine" of the Pastorals is what I call "a doctrine of (about) doctrine." A well-known group of Greek technical terms is used to develop this "doctrine." Since the nature of these terms is "well-known," I shall discuss their basic thrust only very briefly. The focus of my attention will be upon demonstrating why the "doctrine" they represent is especially relevant to the specific purpose of this study.

The basic thrust of those technical terms has been quite well stated by language used to depict "παραθήκη" -- literally: "deposit, property entrusted to another."(37) It has been pointed out, however, that: "The term ["παραθήκη"] belongs in the legal sphere where it emphasizes the integrity of a given definition." (38) The phrase, "integrity of a given definition," reflects the same basic characteristic of this "doctrine of (about) doctrine" Dibelius saw in a more common technical term "ὑγιαίνουσα διδασκαλία" ("sound teaching"): "ein gewisser Rationalismus." (39) Two other technical terms used prominently to develop this "doctrine" are: "ὑγιαίνοντες λόγοι" ("sound words"); and "καλὴ διδασκαλία" ("good teaching"). "καλήν" is also used, at 2 Tim. 1:14, with "παραθήκην." The use of the adjective "καλός" -- and especially that of the progressive participle of "ὑγιαίνω" -- with certain substantives thus provide the most common forms for expressing this "doctrine of doctrine" designating "correct doctrine"(40) ; the doctrine having the "rational" "integrity" suggested by "παραθήκη."

I need cite only three passages involving this "doctrine of doctrine" to indicate why the context in which it often functions is especially relevant to this study. 1) "If you put these instructions before the brethren, you will be a good minister of ...Christ, nourished on the words of the faith and of the good doctrine ["τῆς καλῆς διδασκαλίας"] ....Have nothing to do with godless and silly myths ["μύθους"]."(41) 2) "If any one teaches otherwise and does not agree with the sound words ["ὑγιαίνουσιν λόγοις"] of our Lord Jesus Christ...he...has a morbid craving for controversy and for disputes about words...."(42) 3) "Guard what has been entrusted to you ["τὴν παραθήκην"] . Avoid the godless chatter and...what is falsely called knowledge ["τῆς ψευδωνύμου γνώσεως"]...."(43) Dibelius, of course, cited the latter passage as a possible indication that "γνῶσις" may have been a "discredited word," a reflection of the Pastorals' general anti-Gnostic orientation.(44) It should be apparent that the use of "καλῆς διδασκαλίας," contrasted with "μύθους," and the use of "ὑγιαίνουσιν λόγοις" -- in the context of rejection of those with "a morbid craving for controversy and for disputes about words" -- reflect a similar orientation.

These technical terms were not, of course, created by the writer(s) of the Pastorals. Most of them had long been in secular use, employed to distinguish between "rational" and "silly" ways of thinking.(45) It is significant, however, that the Pastorals consciously employed pre-existing technical terms in service of a broader "doctrine of doctrine" of specific relevance to this study. That is, one of the basic functions of the Pastorals' "doctrine of doctrine" clearly seems to have been to contrast "rational," "sound" doctrine -- doctrine having "integrity" -- with "unsound" ("speculative"), "false knowledge." The "doctrine of (about) doctrine" was thus used against what can only be called "speculative" "Gnostic," or at least "gnosticizing," inquiries representing the type of attitude concerned with matters such as: "knowledge of the Depth (βάθος) of the All"!

The first three standard dogmatic categories used to depict the "content" of "correct Christian doctrine" in the Pastorals are, therefore, irrelevant to the "content" of the "Christian doctrine" of "section A" of Thom. Cont. The fourth category used to describe the Pastorals' "Christian doctrine," one unique to those letters within the New Testament, represents a "doctrine" often used against what must be called, at the least, "gnosticizing" tendencies and the "way of thinking" which would be concerned with: "knowledge of the Depth (βάθος) of the All." It may thus be said that all four categories used to describe the "content" of the "Christian doctrine" of the Pastorals are either irrelevant, or actually opposed, to the basic orientation of the "Christian doctrine" of "section A" of Thom. Cont.!

If the relationship between the "content" of the two versions of "correct Christian doctrine" in question is stated in the reverse manner, the result is even more striking. Every discernible element of the "content" of the version of "Christian doctrine" contained in "section A" of Thom. Cont. is emphatically and specifically rejected by the Pastoral Epistles! This is especially the case with regard to the two clearly most important elements of the "Christian doctrine" of that section.

I have stated that "the most clearly defined point" of the "content" of the "Christian doctrine" of "section A" of Thom. Cont. is the "entirely ascetically oriented point" that one must know that he is "a (bestial) creature...bound to perish unless all one's worldly attachments are denied." The emphatic statement at 1 Tim. 4:2-4 clearly rejects the view that a Christian should consider the created world as intrinsically evil. Any extreme asceticism derived from such a view is, therefore, likewise opposed. "For everything created by God is good...."(46) Therefore, specifically, those "who forbid marriage and enjoin abstinence from foods"(47) are "liars whose consciences are seared ...."(48)

The second most important doctrinal point in the "Christianity" of "section A" of Thom. Cont. is what I have called: "the teaching, that there is one portion of mankind for whom salvation is possible, [and] ...another portion...'the Savior' himself does not even desire saved." This doctrinal point of Thom. Cont., asserting the divine desire that some not be saved, is even more emphatically -- and frequently -- specifically rejected by the Pastorals. I would even suggest that the rejection of such a view about the divine will concerning the scope of salvation actually seems one of the letters' principal purposes! I shall cite, here, just two of the relevant passages. "This is good, and it is acceptable in the sight of God our Savior, who desires all men to be saved and to come to the knowledge of the truth ["εἰς ἐπίγνωσιν ἀληθείας ἐλθεῖν"]."(49) "For the grace of God has appeared for the salvation of all men...."(50)

The only other discernible aspect of the "Christian doctrine" of "section A" of Thom. Cont. consists of the element represented by the phrase: "knowledge of the Depth (βάθος) of the All." I have just shown that the Pastorals' "doctrine of doctrine" was often used precisely in order to combat the sort of "gnostic," or "gnosticizing," "speculation" which would be interested in seeking such types of "knowledge." It should thus be clear beyond a shadow of a doubt that the "content definitions" of the first facet of the meanings of the two formally synonymous technical terms, "ⲡⲥⲟⲟⲩⲛ̄ⲕ̄ⲧⲙⲏⲉ" and "ἐπίγνωσις ἀληθείας," could not

be more radically different. The versions of the "content" of
the "correct Christian doctrine" represented by the two terms
are practically diametrically opposed.

The result is much the same when the "content definitions" of
the second facet of the meaning of those two technical terms are
compared. The actual quality of the "way of life" in which an
"understanding" of "ⲡⲥⲟⲟⲩⲛⲛ̄ⲧⲙⲏⲉ" "necessarily expresses itself"
is, of course, fixed by the "content" of the "correct Christian
doctrine" represented by that phrase in "section A." Its most
crucial element, therefore, reflects the "most clearly defined
point" of the "content" of that doctrine. The "way of life" in
question must be dominated by the most stringently ascetic attempt to shun all the desires -- epitomized by sexual desire --
of one's intrinsically evil physical body. "The Savior" states,
it will be recalled: "'Everyone who seeks the truth from the...
wise One will make himself wings so as to fly, <u>fleeing the lust</u>
(ἐπιθυμία) <u>that scorches the spirits</u> (πνεῦμα) <u>of men.</u>'"(51) As
Turner has succinctly commented: "...the reader is [thus] in-
formed that <u>the central message of the tractate</u> has to do with
the necessity (and wisdom!) of fleeing the fire of sexual lust
which burns in one's body."(52) The strictest asceticism, especially expressed by the rejection of sexual desire, is clearly
the most important characteristic of the actual quality of the
"way of life" expressed by one having an "understanding" of the
"correct Christian doctrine" represented by "ⲡⲥⲟⲟⲩⲛⲛ̄ⲧⲙⲏⲉ."

That "way of life" includes, however, another element which must
not be ignored. It should be clear, from my depiction of the
"content" of the "Christian doctrine" of "section A" of <u>Thom.</u>
<u>Cont.</u>, that the "Christian way of life" includes what can only
be called (my language) : "shunning and despising 'blind men.'"
"The Savior" specifically demands such action of Thomas -- <u>after</u>
he has "already understood" "ⲡⲥⲟⲟⲩⲛⲛ̄ⲧⲙⲏⲉ." Turner, of course,
apparently has interpreted the passage in question quite differently. "One has the obligation to proclaim this condition to
other miserable mortals who have the misfortune to be 'begotten
in the flesh' (<u>141:19-25</u>)."(53) I have already pointed out that
Turner's <u>interpretation</u> of Thomas's questions to "the Savior" at
141,19-25 is very dubious. Those questions seem clearly meant
to set the stage -- <u>not</u> for any "missionary" command -- but for
the <u>prohibition</u> against speaking to "blind men," who are to be
regarded as "beasts."

Turner considered that "obligation" (of "proclamation") : "...
to be the extent of any <u>positive ethical action prescribed in</u>
<u>section A.</u>"(54) If, therefore, one finds no such "obligation"
in that passage, the result is obvious. The actual quality of
the "[Christian] way of life" demanded by an "understanding" of
"ⲡⲥⲟⲟⲩⲛⲛ̄ⲧⲙⲏⲉ" lacks any "positive ethical" dimension whatsoever!
The "content definition" of this second facet of the technical
meaning of "ⲡⲥⲟⲟⲩⲛⲛ̄ⲧⲙⲏⲉ" has, therefore, only two -- negative --
aspects. An "understanding" of "ⲡⲥⲟⲟⲩⲛⲛ̄ⲧⲙⲏⲉ" "necessarily ex-

presses itself" in a "way of life" of: 1) extreme ascetic rejection of all bodily desires; 2) "shunning and despising 'blind men.'"

The "content definition" of the second facet of the meaning of the technical term "ἐπίγνωσις ἀληθείας" in the Pastorals is -- obviously -- radically opposed to the "content definition" of the second facet of the meaning of "ⲡⲥⲟⲟⲩⲛⲛ̄ⲧⲙⲏⲉ" just described. It has already been shown that the Pastorals explicitly reject <u>excessive</u> asceticism as proper to the Christian "way of life." (55) They, of course, also reject <u>excessive</u> worldly "ἐπιθυμία" as proper to the Christian's "way of life." "So shun youthful passions ["ἐπιθυμίας"]...."(56)

<u>Both</u> of these <u>extremes</u> are rejected, however, primarily because each runs contrary to the fundamental thrust of the Christian "way of life" <u>positively</u> enjoined by the Pastorals. The Pastoral Epistles fundamentally advocate the "manner of life,"(57) or "Christian attitude,"(58) characterized by the nearly <u>functionally</u> synonymous technical terms "εὐσέβεια" and "σωφροσύνη." The "way of life" designated by those terms is perhaps best <u>described</u> by the English terms: "<u>moderation</u>"; "restraint"; "<u>self-control</u>."(59) "Moderation" is, perhaps, the one most appropriate English word which could be used to depict the Pastorals' basic view of the proper Christian "way of life."

1 Tim. 2:3-4(60) has already been quoted in another context. It is instructive here, however, to note what is actually designated by "this" ("τοῦτο") which is: "good, and...acceptable in the sight of God our Savior, who desires all men to be saved...." "I urge that supplications...be made for all men, for kings and all who are in high positions, [in order] that ["ἵνα"] <u>we may lead a quiet and peaceable life, godly</u> ["ἐν...εὐσεβείᾳ"] <u>and respectful in every way</u>."(61) The rejection, at 2 Tim. 2:22, of excessive "ἐπιθυμία" (so that one may: "aim at righteousness, faith, love, and peace") is also advocated at Tit. 2:11-12 in the context of the same ethic of "moderation." Furthermore, as is the case at 1 Tim. 2:1-4, the injunction to a life of "moderation" appears in Titus closely linked to an emphatic statement of God's desire for universal salvation. "For the grace of God has appeared <u>for the salvation of all men, training us to renounce irreligion</u> ["ἀσέβειαν"] <u>and...passions</u> ["ἐπιθυμίας"] <u>...to live sober</u> ["σωφρόνως"], <u>upright, and godly</u> ["εὐσεβῶς"] <u>lives in this world</u>...."(62)

This discussion of the "way of life" of "εὐσέβεια-σωφροσύνη," in itself, allows important conclusions to be drawn regarding the relationship between the "content definition" of the second facet of the technical meaning of "ⲡⲥⲟⲟⲩⲛⲛ̄ⲧⲙⲏⲉ" and the "content definition" of the same facet of the technical meaning, in the Pastorals, of "ἐπίγνωσις ἀληθείας." 1) The basic Christian "way of life" advocated by the Pastorals, that life of "moderation," opposes the extreme asceticism which is the almost totally dominant feature of the "Christian way of life" urged in "section A" of Thom. Cont. 2) The Pastorals sometimes advocate that life of "moderation" in the context of emphatic statements of God's desire for universal salvation. Such statements contradict, of course, the only other discernible feature of the "content definition" of the "Christian way of life" in "section A" of Thom. Cont. -- the demand that some men be "shunned and despised" because "the Savior" does not desire their salvation.

Even if Turner is correct, and there are -- certainly "veiled" in my view -- "missionary" injunctions in "section A" of Thom. Cont., that text obviously lacks anything even vaguely resembling the urgent positive missionary charges found, for example, at 2 Tim. 4:2,5. "Preach the word, be urgent in season and out ...convince, rebuke, and exhort, be unfailing...in teaching.... Do the work of an evangelist, fulfill your ministry." The words immediately preceding that charge create, moreover, an almost eschatological context for the injunctions. "I charge you in the presence of God and of Christ Jesus who is to judge the living and the dead, and by his appearing and his kingdom: preach the word...."(63) These injunctions have a tone of urgency and intensity totally lacking in any "missionary" charge to Thomas which might conceivably be present in "section A" of Thom. Cont. It may not be totally coincidental that the language at 2 Tim. 4:3-4 implies that the reason for this urgency involved conflict with, at least "gnosticizing," false teachers! "For the time is coming when people will not endure sound teaching ["ὑγιαινούσης διδασκαλίας"], but having itching ears will accumulate for themselves teachers to suit their own likings, and will turn away from listening to the truth and wander into myths ["μύθους"]." (64)

It is clear that the "content" of the actual quality of the "way of life" necessarily arising from "understanding" the "correct Christian doctrine" represented by "ἐπίγνωσις ἀληθείας" in the Pastorals is radically different from the actual "way of life" arising from a similar "understanding" of "ⲡⲥⲟⲟⲩⲛ̄ⲛ̄ⲧⲙⲏⲉ." The "way of life" enjoined by the Pastorals directly opposes the two discernible aspects of the "way of life" taught in "section A" of Thom. Cont. In "section A" of Thom. Cont., according to my analysis, the "Christian way of life" lacks any positive ethical dimension whatsoever. The Pastorals, to cite just their urgent "missionary ethic," certainly do contain a positive ethical dimension. The "content definitions" of the second facet of the meaning of the formally synonymous technical terms "ⲡⲥⲟⲟⲩⲛ̄ⲛ̄ⲧⲙⲏⲉ" and "ἐπίγνωσις ἀληθείας" are just as radically opposed as were the "content definitions" of the first aspect of their technical meanings.

The analysis of the "content definitions" of the third facet of the technical meaning of these two formally synonymous technical terms will show them to stand in basically the same position of drastic opposition. In "section A" of Thom. Cont., and in the

Pastorals, what is actually involved in "'being saved,'" in "the whole matter of 'soteriology'"? It is useful to divide the analysis of this broad question into that of four more precisely defined questions, the first two of which are closely related. 1) According to the two versions of "correct Christian doctrine" in question, what is "the way to salvation"? 2) What is the actual "method" by which "the Savior" saves? 3) What is considered the "time(table) of salvation"? 4) According to these two versions of "Christian doctrine," "Who can, and/or ought, to be saved"?

It should be clear from what has already been said that, according to the "basic teaching" of "section A" of Thom. Cont., the "way to salvation" involves only two, closely related elements. One must attain, by grasping the revelatory words of "the Savior," knowledge of one's present state, bestial and lustful -- driven by, and captive of, worldly desires. Then, the one who has attained this self-knowledge, and he alone, may seek escape from that state -- by the most strictly ascetic rejection of all fleshly-worldly desires.

The Pastorals' teaching about the actual "way to salvation" has nothing whatsoever in common with "the way" taught in "section A" of Thom. Cont. This is the case primarily because their view on this matter is, overall, in agreement with the basic "gospel" message of the New Testament.(65) That is, the "way to salvation" is by means of the grace and mercy of God displayed and activated by the incarnate, resurrected and exalted Lord Jesus Christ. Ascetic effort is basically irrelevant because men are not saved by their goodness, but by the goodness of God as displayed and enacted in Christ. I quote just two of the passages asserting this fundamental point. "Take your share of suffering for the gospel in the power of God, who saved us and called us with a holy calling, not in virtue of our works but in virtue of his own purpose and the grace...he gave us in Christ Jesus ages ago...."(66) "When the goodness and loving kindness of God our Savior appeared, he saved us, not because of deeds done by us in righteousness, but in virtue of his own mercy...which he poured out upon us richly through Jesus Christ our Savior, so that we might be justified by his grace...."(67)

In the Pastorals, furthermore, God's "grace" and "mercy," never mentioned in the "Christian teaching" of "section A" of Thom. Cont., open the "way to salvation" to those who "believe" -- not to those who "know." "Christ Jesus came into the world to save sinners. And I am the foremost of sinners; but I received mercy ...that in me...Christ might display his perfect patience for an example to those who were to believe in him for eternal life." (68) "Belief" is also, of course, a concept totally alien to the thought world of "section A" of Thom. Cont.

The conclusion to be drawn from this comparison is obvious. The two crucial elements of the "way to salvation" taught in "sec-

tion A" of Thom. Cont. are totally lacking in the teaching of
the Pastorals. According to the Pastorals, there is no need to
gain any special type of "knowledge." There is also no need to
strive, by extreme asceticism, to be saved by escape from a basically evil body and world. On the other hand, the two crucial
elements of the "way to salvation" taught by the Pastorals are
totally alien to the thought of "section A" of Thom. Cont. which
knows nothing of the proclamation of the grace of God as the ultimate "cause" of salvation -- or of the demand that what is required of men is "belief" in this grace. In short, the "content
definitions" of the "way to salvation" derived from the "basic
teachings" of "section A" of Thom. Cont. and of the Pastorals
could hardly be more different!

The second "soteriological" question, that concerning the "method" by which "the Savior" saves, is obviously closely related to
the question about the "way to salvation." It is hardly surprising, therefore, that the teachings of "section A" of Thom.
Cont. and the Pastorals on the "methodology" of "the Savior" are
again radically different.

The definition of that "methodology," according to that section
of Thom. Cont., may be stated quite simply. "The Savior" saves
by imparting the potentially saving knowledge of one's present
dismal state, enslaved by the desires and passions of the world
and body -- imparting that knowledge to those meant to, or capable of, receiving it. He also implicitly, and occasionally
explicitly, urges the appropriate (ascetic) action demanded by
that self-knowledge. These two functions encompass the totality
of the "methodology" of "the Savior" in "section A" of the text
of Thom. Cont.! It is useful, as both a summary of the view of
Thom. Cont. on this matter, and as a means of transition to the
Pastorals' radically different view, to quote Turner's remarks
on the question: "The Savior acts only as revealer and exhorter,
and no other salvific functions, such as are found in the New
Testament, are attributed to him. There seems to be no...under-
standing of Christ as a 'ransom'...no mention of Christ's life
...cross, and Resurrection."(69)

The Pastorals do display some apparent "peculiarities," vis-à-
vis the other canonical New Testament books, in their depiction
of the "methodology" of "the Savior," Jesus Christ. Their view
is, nevertheless, sharply differentiated from that of "section
A" (or "B") of Thom. Cont. by the basic fact that -- like the
rest of the New Testament -- they describe that "methodology"
primarily in terms of historical events related to the life of
Christ. More specifically, the relatively few explicitly "methodological" passages basically depict the cross, the resurrection and the resultant work of the Holy Spirit as the "method"
by which Jesus Christ acted as "the Savior." In the words just
quoted Turner emphasized the total irrelevance of such events
to the "methodology" of "the Savior" in Thom. Cont.

The most important "methodological" statements in the Pastorals are found, without question, at 1 Tim. 2:5-6 and Tit. 2:13-14. They are quite significant -- for several reasons. Both texts take the cross, unmentioned in either section of Thom. Cont., as central to the "method" by which Jesus Christ, "the Savior," saved. Both, however, also interpret the cross in a quite specific way which seems to dominate uniquely, vis-à-vis the rest of the New Testament, the Pastorals' understanding of the cross. That very interpretation, moreover, was specifically noted by Turner as being significant -- because of its absence -- in the ideology of Thom. Cont.: the idea of Christ as a "ransom"!

1 Tim. 2:5-6 contains, not only a technical term "ransom," but also another technical term very closely related to the idea of "ransom." "For there is one God, and...one mediator ["μεσίτης"] between God and men, the man Christ Jesus, who gave himself as a ransom ["ὁ δοὺς ἑαυτὸν ἀντίλυτρον"] for all...."(70) The related passage at Tit. 2:13-14a expresses the same idea of use of a verb belonging to the same word group of which "ἀντίλυτρον" is a member: "...awaiting our blessed hope, the appearing of the glory of our great God and Savior Jesus Christ, who gave himself for us to redeem us ["ἵνα λυτρώσηται ἡμᾶς"] from all iniquity ...."(71)

A discussion of the history of the controversy about the idea of Jesus Christ as a "ransom" is obviously not called for here. It is important, however, since that motif is so prominent in the Pastorals, that the idea of Christ as a "ransom" be correctly understood. "ἀντίλυτρον," which appears in the New Testament only at 1 Tim. 2:6,(72) and the verbal form "λυτρώσηται" which expresses the "same thought"(73) at Tit. 2:14, do seem to dominate uniquely the interpretation of the meaning of the cross in the "Christian doctrine" of the Pastorals. Nevertheless, they express an idea based upon a well known and important Synoptic "saying of Jesus" found at Mark 10:45 (Matt. 20:28).(74) Moreover, in agreement with Büchsel's incisive analysis of "λύτρον-ἀντίλυτρον-λυτρόω,"(75) I take the meaning of the "ransom" saying in the Synoptics -- and of Christ as a "ransom" in the Pastorals -- to be precisely the idea so often rejected (when incorrectly understood): the idea that God "demands" his own son's life as a "substitute" "ransom" ("price of release") for mankind's salvation.(76)

The critical question, however, which has accounted for much of the misunderstanding of Christ as a substitutionary ransom is: What was the content, the nature, of that which had to be "substituted"? Büchsel's discussion of that question is focused on the interpretation of the Synoptic sayings, which fix the meaning of the two "ransom" passages in the Pastorals.(77) He calls attention to the real problem created by the fact that Jesus had dared to offer sinners forgiveness and a new relationship with a holy God, a God who demanded total obedience as the "price" of such forgiveness. The words reported in the Synoptics' "ransom sayings" thus reflect Jesus's perception that he must <u>substitute his own total obedience</u> for the disobedience of the sinners he offered forgiveness. Only by such a "substitution" could the integrity of the Holy God, for whom the "price" of such a forgiveness was total obedience, be protected. Furthermore, Jesus could only be certain that his obedience would be accepted as "total" if he did not stop short of the <u>ultimate</u> sacrifice God could demand, life itself.

Jesus thus "substituted" his own total obedience, <u>in death</u>, as the "price of release" for the disobedient men he had dared offer the forgiveness offered previously only by God himself -- to the totally obedient. Only in this way could Jesus be sure that the new relationship of forgiveness he had made real for sinners would not seem the result of a "cheap grace" which would destroy the holiness of God's demand for total obedience.

> To impart true remission of sins to true sinners, i.e., to men who are chained by their sin in <u>disobedience to God</u>, to declare that now these men are eternally free from...guilt, is something which He alone could do <u>who lifted up...sinners out of the world of their disobedience to God...into the field of His own perfect obedience to God...who did this by creating in the world a place where the full holiness of God would be manifested by the offering up of His own life to God.</u>(78)

The nature of what Jesus "substituted," by his own death as a "substitutionary ransom," ("price of release") was, simply: "total obedience"!

In this context one may see why the technical term "μεσίτης" -- "mediator" -- at 1 Tim. 2:5 is closely related to the "ransom" idea. The "substitutionary" act of Jesus allowed <u>the establishment of a new relationship</u> between men and God. Such action is precisely what Oepke sees as the basic "religious" idea of "mediatorship," the action of one "who arranges business deals and contracts and...<u>brings together those previously unrelated</u>."(79)

There is no doubt that these two complex "ransom" passages thus fix the <u>cross</u> as the decisive event in the Pastorals' depiction of the saving "methodology" of "Christ our Savior." The cross is interpreted, moreover, as an act involving the very "understanding" ("ransom") Turner specifically notes as conspicuous by its absence in <u>Thom. Cont.</u>

The resurrection does not dominate the soteriological doctrine of the Pastorals in the way it does much of the rest of the New Testament. Nevertheless, the resurrection is affirmed in one important passage, and in a context which clearly shows that it is seen as part of the "methodology" of Jesus Christ acting as "the Savior." This fact alone differentiates the soteriological doctrine of the Pastorals from that of <u>Thom. Cont.</u> In that text the most that could be said concerning the resurrection is that, since "the Savior" functions "just prior to the Ascension,"(80) the resurrection might be considered as being "presupposed."

In that "one important passage" it is stated: "Remember Jesus Christ, risen from the dead ["ἐγηγερμένον ἐκ νεκρῶν"], descended from David...preached in my gospel....If we have died with him, we shall also live with him...."(81) Although the resurrection is not <u>directly</u> proclaimed there as a "saving" event, the <u>context</u> clearly suggests that it is to be viewed as such. Jesus Christ, as risen (resurrected), is "preached in my gospel ["τὸ εὐαγγέλιόν μου"]." "εὐαγγέλιον" is a technical term found: "...in our lit. only in the specif. sense [of] God's <u>good news</u> to men...."(82) It is clear that, if Christ as "risen" is preached as part of "God's <u>good news</u> to men," that resurrection is seen as part of the message of the "good news" of "salvation."

The language at 2 Tim. 2:11 is especially significant, not only with regard to the specific point now in question, but for an additional, <u>intrinsically</u> important, reason. "If we have died with him, we shall also live with him...." The relevance of the statement to the specific point in question here is easily discernible. Our "living," that is, our "salvation," is certainly linked to Christ's "living" <u>after</u> having died. It would seem that Christ's resurrection -- living after dying -- thus appears as part of the "method" by which we are given life -- "saved." Also, it has already been shown that the cross, as a "ransom," is viewed as a "method" of salvation in the Pastorals. Therefore, the equation of -- or parallelism between -- <u>dying</u> (the cross) and living (again) stated here is significant. It must strengthen the impression that the resurrection is <u>also</u> viewed as a "method" of salvation. This passage surely, though indirectly, affirms the resurrection as being a part of the "method" by which "the Savior" saves.

The "<u>intrinsically</u> important" point suggested at 2 Tim. 2:11 is to be derived precisely from that equation of, or parallelism between, the cross and resurrection implied there. Many important New Testament passages assert the integrity of the cross and the resurrection as a <u>unitary event</u> in the "method" of salvation. Only at 2 Tim. 2:11 do the Pastorals seem to assert -- and indirectly at that -- this important aspect of the message of the New Testament.

The language at Tit. 3:4b-6 must again be cited as relevant to the analysis of this part of the question regarding the "method" by which "the Savior" saves. That passage is instructive, not only because it again differentiates the teaching of the Pastorals on this particular matter from that found in "section A" of <u>Thom. Cont.</u>, but also because it reinforces the point that the Pastorals -- unlike <u>Thom. Cont.</u> -- fundamentally view Jesus Christ as "the Savior" because he acts as the agent of the Ultimate "Savior," "God the Father." "God our Savior...saved us

...in virtue of his own mercy, by the washing of regeneration and renewal <u>in the Holy Spirit</u>, which he poured out upon us... <u>through Jesus Christ our Savior</u> ["διὰ 'Ιησοῦ Χριστοῦ τοῦ σωτῆρος ἡμῶν"]...."(83) The point of obvious relevance to this particular part of the soteriological analysis is simply that the Holy Spirit -- never mentioned in <u>Thom. Cont.</u> -- is said to play a role in the "method" by which Jesus Christ saves.

I must also stress, however, the striking manner in which this passage -- perhaps as much as any single passage in the Pastoral Epistles -- affirms that Jesus is seen as "the Savior" primarily in his role of servant of the one Holy God. It is clearly indicated at Tit. 3:4b that the initiator of the entire saving act described at Tit. 3:5-6 is God the Father. The Greek of a portion of 3:6b has been quoted because it makes Jesus Christ's role as "Savior" -- involving in this case the "method" of the Holy Spirit -- even more clear in its relationship to the role of God the Father as the Ultimate "Cause of Salvation." In the phrase "διὰ 'Ιησοῦ Χριστοῦ τοῦ σωτῆρος ἡμῶν" "διὰ" must be used with its sense: "of means, instrument, <u>agency</u>...w. gen. of the pers....denoting the personal <u>agent</u>...<u>through</u> (<u>the agency</u> of) <u>by</u>...."(84)

This much at least may now be said, in summary, about the second matter involved in the analysis of "soteriology," a part of that question admittedly not answered in detail or totally unambiguously by the Pastoral Epistles. 1) There is absolutely nothing in the soteriological "methodology" of "the Savior" in "section A" of <u>Thom. Cont.</u> which has anything <u>at all</u> to do with the Pastorals' description of the "method" by which "the Savior" saves. 2) The cross and the resurrection -- no matter how they are interpreted and/or described in the Pastorals -- are still seen as important parts of the "methodology" by which Jesus Christ functions as "the Savior." The Pastorals' teaching on the matter of the "method" by which "the Savior" saves is, therefore, radically differentiated from that of "section A" of <u>Thom. Cont.</u> simply by the fact that <u>historical acts</u> involving the <u>life</u> of "the Savior," a realm of activity irrelevant to either section of <u>Thom. Cont.</u>, are important in the Pastorals. 3) It is also noteworthy that the meaning of the cross is interpreted in the Pastorals primarily in terms of the "ransom" motif, an "understanding" Turner specifically mentions as being conspicuous -- by its absence -- in <u>Thom. Cont.</u> 4) The only other "method" the Pastorals mention in describing God's salvation "methodology" through the "agency" of Jesus Christ as "the Savior," the outpouring of the Holy Spirit through Christ, is, of course, also alien to "section A" (or "B") of <u>Thom. Cont.</u>, a text which knows nothing of the Holy Spirit. Therefore, as was the case with the matter of "the way to salvation," the "content definitions" of the actual "method" by which "the Savior" saves derived from the "basic teachings" of "section A" of <u>Thom. Cont.</u> and the Pastorals have nothing in common whatsoever.

The third question involved in the comparison of "the whole matter of 'soteriology,'" according to the "basic teachings" of the Pastorals and "section A" of Thom. Cont., is that of: the "time (table) of salvation." The "time(table) of salvation" in "section A" of Thom. Cont. may be easily summarized. 1) The all-important decision -- whether or not to accept the saving, revelatory knowledge brought by "the Savior" and to act upon it -- must be made now, "in this world." 2) Nevertheless, salvation itself is necessarily (intrinsically) thought of as something of the future. It can not be achieved "in this world" -- precisely because it consists of a hoped for, necessarily future, escape from one's present bestial bodily condition! 3) One's salvation apparently has nothing whatsoever to do with any past or accomplished action by "the Savior." The "soteriology" of Thom. Cont. totally lacks an "Aorist," or "Perfect-tense," dimension. "The entire tractate views salvation and damnation as an eschatological process, worked out by one's loyalties during his embodied life. Therefore, one needs only to be concerned with the present and the future, but not with the past...."(85)

The point of view in the Pastorals is, again, quite different. The Pastorals' essential "time(table) of salvation" reflects a firm assertion of once and for all time completed acts of God, in Christ, which have made salvation possible. The discussion of the "method" by which "the Savior" saves has surely already made it sufficiently clear that the only basis for the present possibility of salvation is the (historical) past. The "time (table) of salvation" in the Pastorals presupposes at least an "Aorist," perhaps more fundamentally, a "Perfect-tense" situation.

Still, however, the present is, in a basically pragmatic sense, the only relevant time to which the Pastorals speak. It is the time in which, above all else, it is demanded that God's past acts in Christ be proclaimed in order that salvation may be made pragmatically "real," actualized! The crucial past tense "ransom" statement at 1 Tim. 2:5-6 is immediately followed by the words: "For this [proclaiming that past act] I was appointed a preacher and apostle...."(86) Similarly, the emphatic statement at 2 Tim. 1:9-10 that God "saved us and called us...in virtue of his own purpose and the grace which he gave us in Christ Jesus ages ago, and now has manifested through...Christ Jesus who abolished death and brought life and immortality...."(87) is followed by the statement: "For this gospel I was appointed a preacher and apostle and teacher...."(88) The necessity of "belief" -- obviously present "belief" -- in God's act of grace has already been pointed out. The present, therefore, must be seen as the crucial time for the proclamation (preaching) which evokes that "belief," actualizing what God's past acts have made possible. The urgent missionary exhortations at 2 Tim. 4:1-5 noted above should also be taken as a reflection of this aspect of the "time(table) of salvation" in the Pastorals.

The "present-tense" aspect of the Pastorals' view of the "time (table) of salvation" also has at least two other dimensions. 1) Present effort to <u>receive</u> what is preached -- implicit, of course, in the demand <u>for that proclamation</u> -- is also urged directly. "Fight the good fight of the faith; <u>take hold</u> [now] of the eternal life to which you were called...."(89) 2) The implications of the meaning of God's past saving acts for proper daily (present) life -- in one's specific <u>Sitz-im-Leben</u> -- must be recognized and acted upon appropriately. Many of the "bourgeois" ethical demands in the letters appear, if viewed in this context, at least more comprehensible. For example, the exhortation (at 1 Tim. 2:2a) to pray "for kings and all who are in high positions" may be seen, not only as a part of the ethic of "moderation," but also as being a reflection of how that ethic was seen as the proper <u>present</u>, <u>specific</u>, <u>response</u> -- in this world as it is -- to the past saving "ransoming" act in Christ (1 Tim. 2:5-6).

I do not mean to imply that the Pastorals contain <u>no</u> futuristic expectation of some type of fuller consummation of the Christian's existence beyond life "in this world." For example, the "hope of eternal life" is spoken of at Tit. 1:2 and 3:7. One may also cite the striking statement: "I charge you to keep the commandment unstained...<u>until</u> the appearing of our Lord Jesus Christ; and this <u>will be made manifest</u> ["δείξει"] at the proper time...."(90) There is a beyond "this world as it is" expectation in the Pastorals. The shape of this more ultimate hope is not, however, defined clearly in the Pastorals; and it is, <u>most certainly</u>, <u>not stressed</u> as the crucial matter with which one should <u>now</u> be concerned!

It could legitimately be said, therefore, that in both "section A" of <u>Thom. Cont.</u> and the Pastorals the <u>present</u> is the critical time in the "time(table) of salvation," the decisive time upon which actual salvation <u>depends</u>. Nevertheless, this common emphasis upon the present must not be allowed to obscure the radical and basic difference between the <u>overall</u> viewpoints of the Pastorals and "section A" of <u>Thom. Cont.</u> on the "time(table) of salvation." The temporal <u>contexts within which</u> "section A" of <u>Thom. Cont.</u> and the Pastorals view that present as "decisive" could hardly be more different! In <u>Thom. Cont.</u>, although salvation is determined by one's present decision "in this world," it is still seen totally as a state of the <u>future</u>. In the Pastorals, however, the present is only seen as being the "time of salvation," <u>is in fact only made possible</u> as a "decisive" time, because of past and completed acts. The past, however -- as has been pointed out repeatedly -- is totally irrelevant to the possibility of salvation in "section A" of <u>Thom. Cont.</u>

In "section A" of <u>Thom. Cont.</u> the present is crucial <u>only because of the future</u>! In the Pastorals the present is only <u>possible</u> as a crucial time <u>because of the past</u>! Therefore, even though both "section A" of <u>Thom. Cont.</u> and the Pastorals see the present as the "decisive" "time of salvation," their basic overall views of the "time(table) of salvation" -- within the context of which that "decisive" present must be viewed -- are <u>radically</u> different! It is thus clear that, just as was the case with regard to the first two "soteriological" matters discussed, the "content definitions" of the "time(table) of salvation" to be derived from the "basic teachings" of "section A" of <u>Thom. Cont.</u> and the Pastorals are drastically different.

The final soteriological question involved in this analysis is: "Who can, and/or ought, to be saved?" This <u>soteriological</u> question is of extreme importance, for two reasons, to the <u>overall</u> purpose of this study. 1) It is involved, in somewhat differing forms, in the definition of the "content" of the other two facets of the technical meaning of "ⲡⲥⲟⲟⲩⲛ̄ⲛ̄ⲧⲙⲏⲉ" in "section A" of <u>Thom. Cont.</u>: the "correct Christian doctrine" it represents; the "way of life" in which "understanding" that "doctrine" is "expressed." The "correct Christian doctrine" in "section A" of <u>Thom. Cont.</u> includes the teaching that it is not right -- in the view of "the Savior" -- that some men even be given the opportunity to be saved. The "way of life" taught in "section A" of <u>Thom. Cont.</u> includes the "shunning and despising" of such "blind men." Some form of this "soteriological" question thus pervades every aspect of the "content definition" of "ⲡⲥⲟⲟⲩⲛ̄ⲛ̄ⲧⲙⲏⲉ"! 2) The Pastorals' view on this matter, integral to every aspect of the meaning of "ⲡⲥⲟⲟⲩⲛ̄ⲛ̄ⲧⲙⲏⲉ," is <u>unequivocal</u>; and it is <u>diametrically opposed</u> to that of "section A" of <u>Thom. Cont.</u>!

The direct answer of "section A" of <u>Thom. Cont.</u> to this final "soteriological" question may be best stated by simply quoting the words originally used to describe the element of its view of "Christian doctrine" related to this point. "The third and final aspect of the 'content' of the 'Christian doctrine' found in 'section A'...consists of the teaching, that while there is one portion of mankind for whom salvation is possible, there is yet another portion whom 'the Savior' himself does not...<u>desire</u> saved.

The position of the Pastorals on this "soteriological" question should already be clear from what has been said in other contexts. It <u>is</u> "unequivocal"; and it is totally opposed to that derived from the "basic teaching" of "section A" of <u>Thom. Cont.</u> The basic thrust of the teaching of the Pastorals on this matter has been succinctly stated in the words: "God <u>in intention is the Savior of all, not a special class</u>...I Timothy [and the Pastorals as a whole] declares quite clearly that <u>no man stands a priori outside the potential realm of God's redemption</u>."(91) I cite again only two passages, previously quoted in other contexts, as examples of "unequivocal" statements of God's <u>intent</u> to save <u>all</u>. 1) "God our Savior...desires all men to be <u>saved</u> and to come to the knowledge of the truth."(92) 2) "The grace of God has appeared for the salvation of all men...."(93)

1 Tim. 2:5-6, which has been discussed at length in other contexts, is again relevant -- for two reasons -- to this crucial question. 1) It has been suggested that those verses are part of a passage which may well have been conceived primarily as a polemic against "false doctrine." One of the specific elements of the polemic, according to that analysis, was to argue that: "God's will is that <u>all</u> men shall be saved - not just a selected group of Gnostics...."(94) According to that analysis, the type of "false doctrine" opposed in the passage had, as one of its chief tenets, a teaching very like that of "section A" of <u>Thom. Cont.</u> on: "Who can, and/or ought, to be saved?"

2) The dependence of the "ransom" statement ("the man...Jesus, who gave himself as a ransom for all ["ὑπὲρ πάντων"]") upon Mark 10:45 has already been noted. Büchsel suggests, however, in his comparison of the Greek of the two passages, that at 1 Tim. 2:6: "The deviations [from the Greek of the Synoptic saying] are <u>typical of the Past.</u>"(95) He then cites, as an example of such a "typical" Pastoral usage, the substitution for: "the indefinite πολλῶν [in Mark] [of] the <u>expressly universal</u>...πάντων...."(96) Surely the purpose for substituting "the expressly universal" "πάντων" for the "indefinite πολλῶν" of Mark was to stress the <u>universal</u> nature of the salvation God offers in Christ.

In the Pastorals: "No man stands <u>a priori</u> outside the potential realm of...redemption."(97) In "section A" of <u>Thom. Cont.</u> the "blind men," at the very least, do stand "<u>a priori</u> outside the potential realm of...redemption." The answers supplied to this final soteriological question by "section A" of <u>Thom. Cont.</u> and the Pastorals are, obviously, unequivocally and <u>diametrically</u> opposed!

The conclusion to be drawn from the totality of this comparison of the "content definitions" of the two technical terms "ⲡⲥⲟⲟⲩⲛ ⲛ̄ⲧⲙⲏⲉ" and "ἐπίγνωσις ἀληθείας" derived from the "basic teachings" of "section A" of <u>Thom. Cont.</u> and the Pastorals should be quite clear. It is also <u>quite</u> striking. When the two <u>formally synonymous</u> technical terms are defined with regard to the actual "content" of their technical meanings, every aspect of the "content definition" of "ⲡⲥⲟⲟⲩⲛⲛ̄ⲧⲙⲏⲉ" -- as "Christsein" -- is drastically opposed to the corresponding facet of the "content definition" of "ἐπίγνωσις ἀληθείας" -- as "Christsein"!

Chapter III
POSSIBLE HISTORICAL PARALLELS IN GREEK TEXTS

The remarkable nature of the relationship between the technical terms "ⲡⲥⲟⲟⲩⲛⲛ̄ⲧⲙⲏⲉ" and "ἐπίγνωσις ἀληθείας" appears even more striking when placed in the appropriate historical perspective. In this chapter the historical investigation will be concerned with possibly technical philosophical-religious usages, during the first three Christian centuries, of "ἐπίγνωσις ἀληθείας" and any other Greek phrase(s) representing the probable Vorlage of "ⲡⲥⲟⲟⲩⲛⲛ̄ⲧⲙⲏⲉ." The first part of that investigation, therefore, must concern itself with the reconstruction of that Vorlage. In this particular case a reconstruction may be made with an extremely high degreee of probable accuracy.(1)

"ⲛ̄ⲧⲙⲏⲉ" almost certainly represents the translation of a form of "ἀλήθεια." In the Sahidic Coptic version of the New Testament "ⲙⲉ"(2) translates a form of "ἀλήθεια" 106 times and forms of (ten) other Greek terms, none of which are nouns, only sixty-two times.(3) The evidence from that version, cited in a different way, appears even more decisive. "ἀλήθεια," while represented 106 times by a form of "ⲙⲉ," is only translated twice by other Coptic nouns -- one of which is a compound form of "ⲙⲉ." (4) The form "ⲛ̄ⲧⲙⲏⲉ" can not reflect translation of Greek attributive adjective modification.(5) The only two other "statistically likely" Greek terms ("ἀληθής" and "ἀληθινός")(6) can, therefore, be removed from consideration.

Since "ⲛ̄ⲧⲙⲏⲉ" can not represent attributive adjective modification, it is also impossible that "ⲛ̄," in the phrase "ⲛ̄ⲧⲙⲏⲉ," is the linking particle "ⲛ̄-" set before such "Ein Attribut."(7) It almost certainly, therefore, must represent the "ⲛ̄-" particle used to connect a noun to its "Regens" in the Coptic "genitive expression" ("Ausdruck des Genitivs").(8) It seems almost sure, therefore, that the Vorlage of "ⲛ̄ⲧⲙⲏⲉ" consisted of a genitive, singular -- because of the Coptic article used -- (9) form of "ἀλήθεια," that is: "(τῆς) ἀληθείας."

The probability is also almost overwhelming that the Vorlage of "ⲡⲥⲟⲟⲩⲛ" was a form of either "γνῶσις" or "ἐπίγνωσις." The data from the Sahidic version of the New Testament should again be cited first. In this case, however, other evidence will also have to be taken into consideration. In that Sahidic version "ⲥⲟⲟⲩⲛ"(10) translates a form of "γνῶσις" twenty-nine times, a form of "ἐπίγνωσις" nineteen times, "πρόγνωσις" twice, and the adjective "γνωστός" once.(11) The evidence from that version, cited again in the reverse manner, is even more impressive because "ⲥⲟⲟⲩⲛ" is the only Coptic noun ever used to translate either "γνῶσις" or "ἐπίγνωσις."(12)

The evidence from the Sahidic New Testament would thus indicate, "statistically," an approximately 60% likelihood that "ⲡⲥⲟⲟⲩⲛ" represents a form of "γνῶσις," and a 40% likelihood that it reflects a form of "ἐπίγνωσις." In this case, however, one may not consider the New Testament evidence in isolation. The Nag Hammadi texts and the Sahidic Coptic New Testament apparently treat <u>Vorlagen</u> containing the noun "γνῶσις" quite differently. In the Sahidic New Testament both "γνῶσις" and "ἐπίγνωσις" are always translated; neither is ever taken over as a loanword.(13) In Nag Hammadi texts, however, the form "ⲅⲛⲱⲥⲓⲥ" appears quite frequently; but there is no form "ⲉⲡⲓⲅⲛⲱⲥⲓⲥ" to be found in the <u>corpus</u>.(14) I cite as evidence the data from fifteen tractates in Codices II, V and VI which have been published in text editions with reliable indices.(15) Those fifteen texts contain no form "ⲉⲡⲓⲅⲛⲱⲥⲓⲥ." "ⲅⲛⲱⲥⲓⲥ" appears as a loanword fifty-one times; "ⲥⲟⲟⲩⲛ" appears fifteen times.

It seems clear, therefore, that if "γνῶσις" was present in the <u>Vorlage</u> of the part of the Greek of <u>Thom. Cont.</u> in question, it could <u>either</u> have been translated <u>or</u> taken over as a loanword, "ⲅⲛⲱⲥⲓⲥ." If "ἐπίγνωσις" had been present there, however, it would have been <u>translated</u>; and in light of the best available source of evidence, the Sahidic New Testament, almost certainly by a form of "ⲥⲟⲟⲩⲛ." Clearly one may not, therefore, ignore the possibility that "40%" might represent a misleadingly low "statistical" likelihood of the probability that "ἐπίγνωσις" was present in the <u>Vorlage</u> of CG II:138,13. I certainly do not intend to maintain that "ἐπίγνωσις" must have been part of that <u>Vorlage</u>. The argument below needs only presuppose that it is almost certain that the <u>Vorlage</u> of "ⲡⲥⲟⲟⲩⲛ" was a form of <u>either</u> "γνῶσις" or "ἐπίγνωσις." The evidence would surely seem to support such a "presupposition."

It appears quite certain from the context, as well as from the form of "ⲡⲥⲟⲟⲩⲛ," that the Greek noun in question ("ἐπίγνωσις" or "γνῶσις") was in the nominative case,(16) and was singular. (17) Finally, it should be noted that Coptic articular nouns may translate either arthrous, or anarthrous, Greek nouns.(18) I cite only one example of such ambiguity, one brought to mind by Dibelius's association of the language at Heb. 10:26 with the technical term "ἐπίγνωσις ἀληθείας" in the Pastoral Epistles. The arthrous phrase at Heb. 10:26 ("τὴν ἐπίγνωσιν τῆς ἀληθείας") and the anarthrous technical term appearing four times in the Pastorals ("ἐπίγνωσιν ἀληθείας") are translated identically in the Sahidic version of the New Testament, by use of a pair of <u>articular</u> Coptic nouns ("ⲡⲥⲟⲟⲩⲛ ⲛ̄ⲧⲙⲉ")(19) The nouns in the phrase in question in <u>Thom. Cont.</u> (both prefixed with the "definite article") might, therefore, represent translation of a <u>Vorlage</u> which contained either arthrous or anarthrous nouns in the Greek.

It has surely now been demonstrated that there is an overwhelming probability that the <u>Vorlage</u> of "ⲡⲥⲟⲟⲩⲛⲛ̄ⲧⲙⲏⲉ" at CG II:138, 13 consisted of a nominative (singular) noun form, either "(ἡ)

επίγνωσις" or "(ἡ) γνῶσις," and a genitive (singular) noun --
"(τῆς) ἀληθείας." It thus seems that the most probable Vorlage
for the phrase "ⲡⲥⲟⲟⲩⲛⲛ̄ⲧⲙⲏⲉ" would have been either "(ἡ) γνῶσις
(τῆς) ἀληθείας" or "(ἡ) ἐπίγνωσις (τῆς)ἀληθείας." It must be
recalled, however, that -- unlike Greek -- in the Coptic "genitive expression" the genitive noun always follows its "Regens."
(20) It must be kept in mind, in the historical survey to follow, that a Vorlage of (for example) "(τῆς) ἀληθείας (ἡ) γνῶσις"
would, therefore, also have been translated: "ⲡⲥⲟⲟⲩⲛⲛ̄ⲧⲙⲏⲉ."

The results of a survey of the non-Christian Greek religious-
philosophical literature in question may be quite briefly summarized. I find only three examples of apparently technical usage of any of the relevant terms. The first appears in Philo:
"Among the Persians there is an order of the magi who...make research into the facts of nature to gain knowledge of the truth
["πρὸς ἐπίγνωσιν τῆς ἀληθείας"]...."(21) The second appears in
the works of Epictetus, a Stoic (ca. 100 C.E.),(22) who wrote:
"A man has received from nature measures and standards for dis-
covering the truth ["εἰς ἐπίγνωσιν τῆς ἀληθείας"]...."(23) The
final quotation is from Maximus of Tyre(24) who suggested that
Homer's poetry be considered "according to philosophy co-ordi-
nated to the emulation of virtue and the knowledge of the truth
["εἰς ζῆλον ἀρετῆς καὶ ἀληθείας γνῶσιν συντεταγμένον"]."(25)

There seems no real justification for associating any of these
three phrases, in their contexts, with the formal technical definitions of "ἐπίγνωσις ἀληθείας" and "ⲡⲥⲟⲟⲩⲛⲛ̄ⲧⲙⲏⲉ." In his discussion of the relevant New Testament technical usage Bultmann
specifically cites the use of "ἐπίγνωσιν τῆς ἀληθείας" in the
first two passages quoted as representing: "...only formal parallels [to the New Testament usage] ; for here ἐπίγνωσις (τῆς)
ἀληθείας means knowledge of truth or reality in general."(26)
I would even suggest that, at least in the quotation from Philo,
and possibly in the passage from Epictetus, the term "ἐπίγνωσιν
τῆς ἀληθείας" refers to what would now be called "natural scien-
tific knowledge." I find it impossible to fix any exact meaning for "ἀληθείας γνῶσιν" in the third passage quoted. One can
certainly say, however, that the meaning of that phrase -- if it
is indeed used as a technical term by Maximus -- is totally unrelated to that of "ἐπίγνωσις ἀληθείας" in the Pastorals and of
"ⲡⲥⲟⲟⲩⲛⲛ̄ⲧⲙⲏⲉ" in Thom. Cont.

A survey of non-Biblical Christian literature from the period
in question yields only one -- quite possibly very relevant --
example of technical usage of one of the Greek terms under consideration. Hippolytus used the phrase "(ἐν) ἀληθείας γνώσει"
in his anti-Gnostic polemic(27) -- in a context in which it does
appear to fit the formal definitions of "ἐπίγνωσις ἀληθείας" and
of "ⲡⲥⲟⲟⲩⲛⲛ̄ⲧⲙⲏⲉ."

The possible technical meaning of "ἀληθείας γνώσει" is quite intimately related to the position in which it appears (in book

10) within the overall framework of the Refutatio.

> The...plan of the work is...evident. The author intends to
> show the unchristian character of the heresies by proving
> their dependence upon pagan philosophy. For this reason the
> Refutation consists of two [sic] parts. The first...books
> 1-4, deals with the different pagan systems....The second
> part...books 5-9, refutes the heresies by coupling each one
> of the...Gnostic sects with some philosophical or pagan sys-
> tem previously mentioned. The tenth book, after summing up
> the previous exposition, gives a chronology of Jewish his-
> tory and an exposition of the true doctrine.(28)

At the end of the ninth book Hippolytus stresses this final and
"positive" goal of his work, stating clearly that his aim is not
limited to a mere refutation of the heresies described.

> We have considered it reasonable, as a crowning stroke to
> the entire work, to introduce the discourse (already men-
> tioned) concerning the truth, and to furnish our delinea-
> tion of this in one book, namely the tenth. Our object is,
> that the reader, not only when made acquainted with...those
> who...presumed to establish heresies, may regard with scorn
> their idle fancies, but also, when brought to know the power
> of the truth, may be placed in the way of salvation....(29)

In the last book of his treatise, after summarizing both the description of the "sources" of heresy found in books 1-4 and the
actual descriptions of them in books 5-9, Hippolytus's entire
work is therefore climaxed -- after the "chronology of Jewish
history" -- by a final section containing his version of "correct Christian doctrine," the "way to salvation"!

It is in this context that the crucial six lines (in the Greek
text used) containing "ἀληθείας γνώσει" appear, the lines which
are the key to that concluding systematic statement of the version of "THE DOCTRINE OF THE TRUTH"(30) taught by Hippolytus.
I offer this quite literal translation of that section of the
Greek in Migne as the basis for my exposition of the technical
meaning of "ἀληθείας γνώσει."

> Therefore, having grasped this [the antiquity of the worship
> of the true God found in the "Jewish history"] -- Greeks,
> Egyptians, Chaldeans, and every race of man -- learn what
> [is] that [which is of] God and the well-ordered creation
> of this from us, the friends of God ["τῶν φίλων τοῦ θεοῦ"],
> trained -- not in boastful word -- but in the knowledge of
> the truth ["ἐν ἀληθείας γνώσει"] and in the practice of mod-
> eration ["σωφροσύνης"]....(31)

It can be shown with considerable probability that the phrase
"ἀληθείας γνώσει," as used in this context by Hippolytus, does
indeed fit the identical formal definitions which have been al-

ready suggested for the technical terms "ἐπίγνωσις ἀληθείας" and "ⲡⲥⲟⲟⲩⲛ̄ⲛ̄ⲧⲙⲏⲉ."

It should be almost self-evident that the term represents the first facet of that formal definition, that it certainly represents an "understanding" of "correct Christian doctrine." The primary purpose of the passage translated clearly is to <u>contrast</u> "the friends of God," the "orthodox" Christians who are characterized by the fact that they are "trained" "in the knowledge of the truth," with the Gnostic heretics who are "trained" in the "boastful" speculative systems previously described at great length by Hippolytus. Lampe cites this very passage as an example of "γνῶσις": "freq. <u>identified with Christian doctrine</u>... <u>sometimes called</u> γ...ἀληθείας...opp. Gnost. fancies, Hipp. <u>haer.</u> <u>10.31</u> (...M.16.3446C)....(32) Since the "friends of God" are trained "ἐν ἀληθείας γνώσει," they may urge "every race of man" to "learn" from them "what the nature of God is, and what His well-arranged creation."(33) Although those words are a rather free translation of the Greek, they do convey, surely, its basic meaning; and they must be seen as a representation of important elements of the "correct Christian doctrine" which may be taught by those "trained" in it, that is, those "trained" "ἐν ἀληθείας γνώσει"!

It is equally apparent that this "understanding" of the "correct Christian doctrine" represented by "ἀληθείας γνώσει": "necessarily expresses itself in one's way of life." These "friends of God" are: "...trained not in boastful word but in the knowledge of the truth and in the practice of moderation ["σωφροσύνης"] ...." A life of "σωφροσύνη" is obviously meant to be taken as intimately related to, indeed almost as being a part of, one's "training" in "the knowledge of the truth." Clearly a "way of life" of "σωφροσύνη" is thus associated by Hippolytus with the "understanding" of "correct Christian doctrine" represented by "ἀληθείας γνώσει." It, therefore, seems quite evident that the phrase "ἀληθείας γνώσει," as used by Hippolytus, represents the first two formally-defined aspects of the technical meaning of "ἐπίγνωσις ἀληθείας" in the Pastorals and of "ⲡⲥⲟⲟⲩⲛ̄ⲛ̄ⲧⲙⲏⲉ" in "section A" of <u>Thom. Cont.</u> To be "trained" "ἐν ἀληθείας γνώσει" is to have an "understanding" of Hippolytus's version of "correct Christian doctrine," an "understanding" which also "necessarily expresses itself in one's way of life," a "way of life" of "σωφροσύνη."(34)

This same "understanding" also clearly seems: "intimately related to 'being saved.'" The "CONCLUDING ADDRESS,"(35) which follows the full exposition of the "content" of "correct Christian doctrine" contained in the final sections of book 10, clearly implies such a relationship. After he has thus outlined the details of his version of that "doctrine" Hippolytus exhorts the reader: "Do not devote your attention to the fallacies...<u>but to</u> <u>the...truth</u>. And <u>by means of this knowledge</u> [that is, "knowledge of the truth"] <u>you shall escape</u>...<u>judgment</u>...[and] <u>hell's</u>

<u>eternal lake of fire</u>...."(36) It is obvious that Hippolytus saw an "intimate relationship" between accepting "correct Christian doctrine" -- which is represented by "ἀληθείας γνώσει" -- (37) and escape from "judgment," that is, "being saved."

This association of being "trained" in "ἀληθείας γνώσει" with "being saved" is also indicated in a more subtle fashion -- and, in this case, in the immediate context in which "the knowledge of the truth" appears. Those "trained...in the knowledge of the truth" are referred to as: "the friends of God ["τῶν φίλων τοῦ θεοῦ"]." There is considerable evidence that, in the <u>Jewish-Christian</u> tradition, the epithet "friend of God" was used as a designation for "one who is saved."

At Jas. 2:23 Abraham is called "friend of God" ("φίλος θεοῦ") in a context which makes that term the functional equivalent of a designation for "the one who is saved." It is stated there, obviously echoing Gen. 15:6, that: "The scripture was fulfilled which says, 'Abraham believed God, and it was reckoned to him as righteousness'; and he was called the friend of God." Stählin's discussion of the context created by the allusion to Gen. 15:6 clearly suggests -- although not explicitly stating -- an association of "friend of God" with "one who is saved." "The meaning of φίλος θεοῦ is...close to 'he who is just through faith'." That is to say: "Abraham is <u>the man who is loved and chosen by God</u>."(38)

The statement at Jas. 2:23, besides echoing Gen. 15:6, probably should also be interpreted in the context of Jub. 19:9 and 30:30 where Abraham is called a "friend of God." That is, the language at Jas. 2:23 may be taken as a reference to that: "...use in the Book of Jubilees (Chs. 19,30) of the expression 'written down as a friend of God,' in the sense of '<u>having been granted salvation</u>'...."(39) Since this tradition associating being a "friend of God" with "being saved" is of <u>Jewish</u> origin, it <u>may</u> not be coincidental that the passage in question from Hippolytus is immediately preceded by his "chronology of Jewish history" meant to show the great antiquity of the worship of the one true God. That "chronology," furthermore, begins with statements about <u>Abraham's</u> departure from Haran.(40)

Hippolytus's reference to those "trained...in the knowledge of the truth" as "the friends of God" seems, therefore, to support the relationship between "being saved" and being "ἐν ἀληθείας γνώσει" <u>clearly</u> suggested by his remarks in the "CONCLUDING ADDRESS." The phrase in question does seem to represent the third and final facet of the formally-defined technical meanings of "ἐπίγνωσις ἀληθείας" and "ⲡⲥⲟⲟⲩⲛⲏ̄ⲧⲙⲏⲉ." "ἀληθείας γνώσει" does serve to represent an "understanding" of "correct Christian doctrine" "intimately related to 'being saved.'" That term, as it is used by Hippolytus in his <u>Refutatio Omnium Haeresium</u> at 10.31, defined purely formally as a technical term, thus appears to be synonymous with the purely formal technical definitions of "ἐπίγνωσις ἀληθείας" and of "ⲡⲥⲟⲟⲩⲛ̄ⲧⲙⲏⲉ" -- "Christsein."

To what extent, however, do the "basic teachings" Hippolytus attacks correspond to the "basic teaching" of "section A" of Thom. Cont.? This question must be asked to determine how similar any heretical version of "Christsein" opposed by Hippolytus's version of "Christsein" ("ἀληθείας γνώσει") might have been to the version of "Christsein" represented by the "content definition" of "ⲡⲥⲟⲟⲩⲛ̄ⲧⲙⲏⲉ." 1) It could be said that in some quite significant ways the composite picture presented by the various heretical teachings Hippolytus described would be similar to that presented by the "basic teaching" of "section A" of Thom. Cont. -- and, of course, thus dissimilar to the "basic teaching" of the Pastorals. 2) That "composite" would also differ in fairly significant ways -- primarily in the relative emphasis placed upon elements -- from the teaching of "section A" of Thom. Cont. 3) Finally, some of the teachings Hippolytus describes are totally absent from "section A" of Thom. Cont.

The teachings portrayed by Hippolytus are (taken overall) similar to the teaching of "section A" of Thom. Cont. in at least three respects. 1) Hippolytus basically characterizes his opponents as "speculators," men seeking and devising "esoteric" doctrine -- the way of thinking reflected in "section A" of Thom. Cont. by the desire for "knowledge of the Depth (βάθος) of the All." I cite two examples. He writes, initially, that he will: "...compare each heresy with the system of each speculator... to show that the earliest champion of the heresy availing himself of these...theories...impelled from these into worse, [and] has constructed his own doctrine."(41) Subsequently, in a quite typical statement, he asserts: "There are...among the Gnostics diversities of opinion; but we have decided that it would not be worth while to enumerate the silly doctrines....Even those... of a more serious turn...have derived their systems of speculation from the Greeks...."(42)

2) Hippolytus sometimes rebukes the heretics for teaching an excessively ascetic way of life. I again cite two examples. He attacks Marcion in this fashion: "You forbid marriage, the procreation of children, (and) the abstaining from meats which God has created for participation by the faithful, and those that [sic] know the truth."(43) The "Encratites" are attacked for:

> ...abstaining from animal food, (and) being water-drinkers, and forbidding to marry, and devoting themselves during the remainder of life to habits of asceticism....They do not attend unto the words spoken against them through the Apostle Paul. Now he, predicting the novelties that were to be... introduced...by certain (heretics), made a statement thus: 'The Spirit speaketh expressly, In [sic] the latter times certain will depart from sound doctrine...having their own conscience seared with a hot iron, forbidding to marry, to abstain from meats, which God has created to be partaken of

with thanksgiving by the faithful, and those who know the
truth; because every creature of God is good, and nothing
is to be rejected which is received with thanksgiving....
(44)

It is clear, therefore, that Marcion, and the vaguely and very
briefly described "Encratites," were strongly ascetic with regard to both sexual activity and diet. The "Encratites" -- as
"water-drinkers" -- apparently also represented the "wine-re-
jecting" aspect of the false teaching opposed in the Pastorals
by the positive injunction: "No longer drink only water, but use
a little wine...."(45) Both Marcion and the "Encratites" are
thus attacked by Hippolytus because they adhered to the most important element of the "basic teaching" of "section A" of <u>Thom.
Cont.</u>, an extreme asceticism. It is in this context that parts
of 1 Tim. 4:1-5 are quoted by Hippolytus against both Marcion
and the "Encratites"!

What has just been said about Hippolytus's attacks upon the extreme asceticism of some of those he opposed demands, for two
reasons which should be obvious, an excursus at this point. 1)
Both Marcion and the "Encratites" apparently held some version
of the "most clearly defined" (ascetically-defined) aspect of
the "Christian doctrine" -- <u>and</u> "way of life" -- derived from
the "basic teaching" of "section A" of <u>Thom. Cont.</u> and represented by "ⲡⲥⲟⲟⲩⲛ̄ⲧⲙⲏⲉ." 2) Hippolytus attacks both Marcion and
the "Encratites" by quoting parts of the Pastoral text so often
evoked in the preceding analysis showing the diametric opposition between those two aspects of the "basic teaching" of "section A" of <u>Thom. Cont.</u> and the corresponding aspects of the Pastorals' teaching. It must be made clear, therefore, that it is
impossible to argue that either of those heresies ("Marcionism"
or the views of the "Encratites") represents the "basic teaching" of "section A" of <u>Thom. Cont.</u> Other important elements of
that "basic teaching," which determines the version of "Christsein" represented by "ⲡⲥⲟⲟⲩⲛ̄ⲧⲙⲏⲉ," are <u>not</u> to be found in the
views of Marcion or of the "Encratites"! The orthodox view of
"Christsein" (as "ἀληθείας γνώσει") held by Hippolytus was not,
therefore, opposed to heretical views of "Christsein" held by
either Marcion or the "Encratites" identical to that represented
by the "content definition" of "ⲡⲥⲟⲟⲩⲛ̄ⲧⲙⲏⲉ."

There is, first of all, no evidence in Hippolytus's description
of the "Encratites" that they even held to the other elements of
the "content" of the "correct Christian doctrine" contained in
the "basic teaching" of "section A" of <u>Thom. Cont.</u> He does not
picture the "Encratites" as being concerned with "esoteric" matters such as "the Depth (βάθος) of the All," or as teaching that
the divine will did not even <u>desire</u> the salvation of a portion
of mankind. It is not surprising, in light of what <u>is</u> known a-
bout the "Encratites," that Hippolytus does little more than attack their extreme asceticism. The term "Encratite" was used
very loosely: "in the Christian heretic-histories to [designate]

certain sectaries, who abstained from animal food, intoxicating drinks, and sexual intercourse."(46) That is, the term was just : "applied to several groups of early Christians who carried... ascetic practice and doctrine to extremes...."(47) Therefore, the "Encratites" attacked by Hippolytus probably simply represent "Christians" espousing an extreme asceticism common to many sects throughout religious history.

The "Encratites" can not, certainly, be at all identified with any known group of "gnostic speculators." Absolutely the most that has been said of any such tendency on their part is: "<u>Nor can they be lumped together with the Gnostics</u>, which, however, does not mean that Encratites <u>here and there</u> may not have represented Gnostic teachings."(48) Hippolytus himself, as already indicated -- in a work basically directed against "Gnostic speculators" -- never condemns the "Encratites" for any type of such "Gnostic" speculation. His polemic against them is directed <u>entirely</u> against their self-righteous, extremely ascetic, "way of life." There is no reason, therefore, to take Hippolytus's quotation from 1 Timothy attacking the "Encratites" as representing anything more than polemic "prooftexting" against a "heretical" (ascetic) "way of life" somewhat similar to that attacked by the Pastorals.

In summary, only three statements need be made here about the "Encratites" attacked by Hippolytus. 1) They represented an extreme asceticism which has been common to many religious groups. 2) Some "Encratites" may have had affinities with "Gnosticism" -- although Hippolytus does <u>not</u> charge the "Encratites" with any type of "gnostic speculation." 3) Nothing is known about the "doctrine" of the "Encratites" on the matter of whom the divine will desires to be saved. There thus seems no reason whatsoever to <u>identify</u> whomever it was Hippolytus attacked as "Encratites" with the group responsible for "section A" of <u>Thom. Cont.</u> and its "basic teaching"!

Much more, of course, is known about Marcion's views than about those of the "Encratites." Precisely what we do know about his "heretical teaching" makes it very clear that, while he did advocate the type of extreme asceticism for which he was attacked by Hippolytus, he certainly could <u>not</u> be charged with "esoteric speculation" which would be concerned with such matters as "the Depth (βάθος) of the All" -- or with any teaching stressing the necessity, let alone the desirability, of the damnation of part of mankind. As was the case with the "Encratites," Marcion's version of just the "content" of "correct Christian doctrine" can not, therefore, be identified with that found in the "basic teaching" of "section A" of <u>Thom. Cont.</u>

Marcion can be <u>associated with</u> some figures who might be called "speculators." He may have originally gained his idea of the necessity of distinguising the God of the Old Testament from the God who was the Father of Jesus Christ from Cerdo: "who had a certain connexion with the Gnostics...."(49) To whatever extent Marcion was actually indebted to the thought of Empedocles, as Hippolytus charges,(50) he would have thus been influenced by a "speculator." The theories of Empedocles would surely have to be called "conjectural," or "speculative."(51)

Marcion's own basic "way of thinking" was -- it is generally accepted -- radically contrary, however, to any such "esoteric," "speculative" orientation. "He has often been reckoned among the Gnostics, but it is clear he would have had little sympathy with their mythological speculations."(52) "Marcion's teaching is especially remarkable for its lack of interest in metaphysical questions."(53) "He was not interested in religious philosophy...."(54) "Marcion's theology differed from the Gnostic in excluding any doctrine of aeons, and indeed, <u>any element... not...derived from his interpretation of the...scriptures.</u>"(55) "He believed in salvation by faith rather than by gnosis...." (56)

Marcion's lack of interest in such "esoteric speculation" would seem a quite logical consequence of other aspects of his basic religious intent and orientation -- the most important of which has already been suggested. That is: "Marcion's thought concerns itself entirely with the religious records of the Jews and the Christians."(57) While one of the key elements of Marcion's "heresy" was his view of scripture, it must still be stressed that scripture, at least as he interpreted it -- not esoteric revelation -- was the basis of "Christian doctrine" for Marcion. The second relevant aspect of his religious orientation to be noted is simply that Marcion's: "...main interest was <u>not speculative</u> or theoretical, <u>but religious and practical.</u>"(58) The very asceticism for which Hippolytus attacked him should actually be seen as one of the most important manifestations of this "religious and practical" thrust of Marcion's teaching.

While Marcion may thus have had some contact with the thought of men who would be called "speculators," it is certainly quite impossible to charge Marcion himself with any excessive interest in "esoteric speculation" concerning matters such as "the Depth (βάθος) of the All."

Marcion <u>most certainly</u> can not be accused of the teaching, that of "the Savior" in "section A" of <u>Thom. Cont.</u>, that the salvation of some is not the divine <u>desire</u>! The crucial aspect of Marcion's teaching which was considered "heretical" consisted, of course, precisely of the view that the New Testament God, who was totally a God of grace desiring the salvation of <u>all</u>, could not be the <u>same God</u> as the stern law-giver of the Old Testament. "In theology Marcion's main assertion was that the just God of the law and of the OT generally <u>was other than and inferior to the God revealed in Jesus</u>...the <u>chief</u> attribute of the latter <u>being goodness or loving kindness.</u>"(59) "Marcion's central thesis was that the Christian Gospel was wholly a Gospel of Love to the absolute exclusion of the law. This doctrine...led him to reject the OT completely. The Creator God...revealed in the OT...as wholly a God of Law, had nothing in common with the God of Jesus Christ."(60) "Marcion taught that there were two gods, proclaiming that the stern, lawgiving, creator God of the Old Testament rivals the good, merciful God of the New Testament." (61) To state the matter in a way which makes Marcion's view "sound" peculiarly like the view of the Pastorals(62) : "He [the God who was the Father of Jesus Christ] wishes to be merciful to sinners and to free all from...the God of the Jews."(63) It certainly can not be said that Marcion accepted the view that the divine will does not desire the salvation of all!

It should now be abundantly clear that no view of "Christsein" derived from any known "basic teaching" of the "Encratites," and certainly no view of "Christsein" derived from Marcion's "basic teaching," would be the same as the view of "Christsein" derived from the "basic teaching" of "section A" of Thom. Cont. and represented by the "content definition" of the term "ⲡⲥⲟⲟⲩⲛ̄ⲛ̄ⲧⲙⲏⲉ." The basic point of this excursus has surely been demonstrated. "The orthodox view of 'Christsein' (as 'ἀληθείας γνώσει') held by Hippolytus was not, therefore, opposed to heretical views of 'Christsein' held by either Marcion or the 'Encratites' identical to that represented by the 'content definition' of 'ⲡⲥⲟⲟⲩⲛ ⲛ̄ⲧⲙⲏⲉ.'"

3) Hippolytus sometimes attacks his opponents for advocating a teaching at least very similar to the classic Gnostic doctrine of the division of mankind -- by nature -- into three groups: the pneumatic; the psychic; the hylic. "These allege that there are three kinds of existence - angelic [that is, "pneumatic"], psychical, and earthly [that is, "hylic"]; and that there are three churches...and that the names of these are - chosen, called, and captive."(64) The teaching thus described certainly is in accord with the teaching in "section A" of Thom. Cont. that there is at least a portion of mankind who, not only can not, but should not, be saved.

The composite picture presented by the teachings described by Hippolytus, if those teachings were taken as representing one "heresy" -- which even he does not allege -- would still differ somewhat from the teaching of the group responsible for "section A" of Thom. Cont. There is, first of all, a considerable discrepancy between the emphases each places upon the elements they would have in common. In "section A" of Thom. Cont. the "doctrinal" element concerned with the desire for "esoteric knowledge" is obviously much less important than the element of its "Christian doctrine" concerning the necessity for self-knowledge of one's bestial, lustful nature. The teachings Hippolytus attacks, however, are -- overall -- basically described as being "wrong" because they consisted of extremely complex, esoteric and arrogant speculative systems of exotic doctrine. He states initially: "They have styled themselves Gnostics, alleging that they alone have sounded the depths of knowledge."(65) Systems, such as that he attributes to Basilides, are described as being so complex(66) that it is impossible for me to attempt a summary here. It has even been said that Hippolytus probably did not rely on "forged documents" for his descriptions of the heresies because: "forgery is unlikely in the case of so speculative a system as that, e.g., of Basilides."(67) While Hippolytus does, therefore, sometimes deprecate the asceticism of his opponents, that aspect of his polemic is clearly subordinate to his attack upon the "speculative" nature of the various "heresies." Within "section A" of Thom. Cont., however, an extreme ascetic point of view (not its "speculative" teaching) dominates almost completely both its version of "Christian doctrine" and the "way of life" in which "understanding" that doctrine "expresses itself."

Furthermore, at least one -- and possibly two -- of the elements involved in any composite picture of the heretical teachings attacked by Hippolytus are (is) lacking totally in "section A" of Thom. Cont. 1) While Hippolytus most frequently deprecates his opponents' "way of life" because of its ascetic nature, there are also examples of attacks upon the heretics' "way of life" because it featured licentiousness, or eroticism! Any such type of attack would be, of course, inconceivable against the group responsible for the "basic teaching" of "section A" (or "section B") of Thom. Cont.! The most striking example of such an anti-erotic polemic in Hippolytus constitutes a major aspect of his attack upon Simon Magus -- certainly, according to Hippolytus, one of the principal heretics. Simon is charged with having had erotic relations with a "reincarnation" of "Helen of Troy," during which he "enjoyed her person," so that: "those who become followers of this imposter...indulge in similar practices, and irrationally allege the necessity of promiscuous intercourse." (68) 2) It has already been pointed out that Hippolytus attacks a doctrine which is, at the least, very similar to the classic Gnostic doctrine of the division of mankind -- by nature -- into three groups: the "pneumatic"; the "psychic"; the "hylic." As I have already stated,(69) despite Krause's assertions, I do not find that teaching clearly or fully formulated in Thom. Cont.

This discussion should have clearly established six points. 1) There are significant similarities between the composite picture which could be constructed from the plethora of heretical teachings described by Hippolytus and the "basic teaching" of "section A" of Thom. Cont. 2) Even such a "composite" would still also differ, however, from the "basic teaching" of "section A" with regard to the relative emphasis placed upon the elements held in common. 3) At least one, and possibly two, significant element(s) of the teachings attacked by Hippolytus can not be found anywhere in "section A" of Thom. Cont. 4) It is impossible, therefore, to identify the rather simplictic "basic teaching" of "section A" of Thom. Cont. with even the teaching of a "composite heresy" constructed from Hippolytus's actual descriptions of the thirty-three heresies he attacks. 5) The "basic teaching" of "section A" of Thom. Cont. most certainly can not be identified with any one of the individual heresies described by Hippolytus.(70) 6) It is also, therefore, impossible to equate completely the version of "Christsein" derived from the "basic teaching" which determines the "content definition" of "ⲡⲥⲟⲟⲩⲛⲛ̄ⲧⲙⲏⲉ" with any heretical version of "Christsein" opposed by Hippolytus's orthodox version of "Christsein," possibly represented by "ἀληθείας γνώσει."

That citation from Hippolytus is the only example I have been able to find, in the Christian non-Biblical literature of the first three centuries, of possibly technical usage of a genitive singular form of "ἀλήθεια" combined with either "ἐπίγνωσις" or "γνῶσις." It seems quite unlikely, therefore, that "the knowledge of the truth" was a widely used technical term in the Greek religious-philosophical literature extant when the Vorlage of Thom. Cont. was composed.

Only one more matter needs to be considered before concluding this survey of possibly relevant Greek literature. "γνῶσις," modified by either "ἀληθής" or "ἀληθινός," was used fairly frequently in anti-Gnostic polemics to represent the "true gnosis" of "orthodox" Christianity. Irenaeus, to cite just one example, used the phrase "Γνῶσις ἀληθής ἡ τῶν ἀποστόλων διδαχή" in such a context.(71) It has already been explained, however, why Coptic syntax prohibits the possibility that "ⲛ̄ⲧⲙⲏⲉ" represents translation of Greek attributive adjective modification.(72) Therefore "ⲡⲥⲟⲟⲩⲛⲛ̄ⲧⲙⲏⲉ" can not refer to the Gnostic's "true knowledge" in the sense Irenaeus and others used Greek terms such as "γνῶσις ἀληθής" to indicate orthodox "true knowledge."

Chapter IV
POSSIBLE PARALLELS IN NAG HAMMADI TEXTS

The establishment of the appropriate historical perspective for consideration of the possible implications of the relationship between "ⲡⲥⲟⲟⲩⲛⲛ̄ⲧⲙⲏⲉ" and "ἐπίγνωσις ἀληθείας" must, of course, also involve a survey of the Nag Hammadi literature. Although the result of that survey of the corpus suggests only three Coptic phrases of possible relevance, the contexts in which those phrases appear require that they be examined at some length. In each case the Coptic almost certainly represents a Vorlage of "(ἡ) γνῶσις (τῆς) ἀληθείας."

Two of the three possibly relevant phrases appear in logion 110 of The Gospel of Philip.(1) It could be argued that the term "ⲧⲅⲛⲱⲥⲓⲥⲛ̄ⲧⲙⲉ" ("the knowledge [γνῶσις] of the truth")(2) and the term "ⲧⲅⲛⲱⲥⲓⲥⲛ̄ⲧⲁⲗⲏⲑⲉⲓⲁ" ("the knowledge [γνῶσις] of the truth [ἀλήθεια]")(3) function together in logion 110 to establish "the knowledge of the truth" as an emphatic technical term having the same formally-defined meaning as "ⲡⲥⲟⲟⲩⲛⲛ̄ⲧⲙⲏⲉ" and "ἐπίγνωσις ἀληθείας"! For the purposes of this analysis the relevant part of the logion should be divided into three sections.

The interpretation of the first section (77,15b-18) presents no real problems. "The one who has the knowledge (γνῶσις) of the truth ["ⲧⲅⲛⲱⲥⲓⲥⲛ̄ⲧⲙⲉ"] is free (ἐλεύθερος); but [or "and"] (δέ) the free one (ἐλεύθερος) does not sin because (γάρ) the one who sins is the slave of sin."(4) While the language almost certainly echoes John 8:32-32, the logic of the statement is clear in itself. The one having "ⲧⲅⲛⲱⲥⲓⲥⲛ̄ⲧⲙⲉ" is free, that is, not a "slave." The one who sins becomes "the slave of sin." One having "ⲧⲅⲛⲱⲥⲓⲥⲛ̄ⲧⲙⲉ," and thus being free of all slavery, can not, therefore, sin; for sinning must result in "slavery."

If "ⲧⲅⲛⲱⲥⲓⲥⲛ̄ⲧⲙⲉ" at CG II: 77,16 is thus interpreted -- and seen as a technical term -- its formal definition clearly reflects the same three facets of technical meaning found in the formal definitions of "ἐπίγνωσις ἀληθείας" and "ⲡⲥⲟⲟⲩⲛⲛ̄ⲧⲙⲏⲉ" outlined initially. 1) Possessing it, "understanding" it, gives freedom -- freedom from sin and slavery to sin. Clearly, therefore, the term represents an "understanding" which is "intimately related to 'being saved.'" 2) Since the one with an "understanding" of "ⲧⲅⲛⲱⲥⲓⲥⲛ̄ⲧⲙⲉ" does not sin, that "understanding" thus obviously also is one which "necessarily expresses itself in one's way of life." 3) Finally, since Gos. Phil. must certainly be taken as a "Christian-Gnostic" text,(5) "the knowledge (γνῶσις) of the truth" must represent -- by definition -- an "understanding" of "correct Christian doctrine."

In the second section (77,19-20a) it is stated that: "The truth (ἀλήθεια) is the mother, but (δέ) the knowledge (γνῶσις) is the

father." This section is not <u>directly</u> involved in explicating
the meaning of the technical term(s) in question. It, however,
may have been intended to make a point which will be very perti-
nent to another aspect of the discussion involving the possible
relevance of this passage to the larger question at hand. That
is, the language of these lines seems to suggest that the "be-
getting" of any "free" child possessing "the knowledge of the
truth," and all that term connotes in the context of 77,15b-18,
demands the <u>union</u> of <u>two</u> parents: "the knowledge"; "the truth."
In this logion, if that is the case, then neither of those two
terms may be taken as having real meaning in isolation. The <u>en-
tire phrase</u> -- "the knowledge of the truth" -- must always be
taken as a unit to discover any meaning.

It is not difficult to see why "ⲧⲁⲗⲏⲑⲉⲓⲁ" is specified as being
"the mother," and "ⲧⲅⲛⲱⲥⲓⲥ" as "the father." In many Gnostic
texts -- and most certainly in <u>Gos. Phil.</u> -- the "Holy Spirit"
is spoken of as being feminine.(6) In the Fourth Gospel, obviously well known to the writer(s) of <u>Gos. Phil.</u>,(7) one sometimes finds the, at least functional, equation of "the (Holy)
Spirit" and "the Spirit of Truth."(8) It is not difficult, with
these factors in mind, to account for the additional "logical"
step to the statement that "ⲧⲁⲗⲏⲑⲉⲓⲁ" is "the mother."

The identification of "the father" as "ⲧⲅⲛⲱⲥⲓⲥ" presupposes the
Gnostic commonplace that the "highest Father" is deeply hidden
-- revealed only through Ultimate <u>Gnosis</u>. That very commonplace
is reflected, moreover, elsewhere <u>in Gos. Phil.</u> "When we were
Hebrews we were orphans and had only <u>our mother</u>, but when we be-
came Christians we had both father and mother."(9) That is, in
this "Christian-<u>Gnostic</u>" text, a "saved Christian" possesses --
as opposed to a "Hebrew orphan" -- the Ultimate saving "γνῶσις"
-- referred to as "father." The language in <u>Gos. Phil.</u> at 52,21
-24 thus also states more directly what is suggested in logion
110. "The saved one," "the free one," has <u>two</u> parents: "father"
and "mother."

The third relevant section of the logion (77,20b-29), in which
the term "ⲧⲅⲛⲱⲥⲓⲥⲛ̄ⲧⲁⲗⲏⲑⲉⲓⲁ" appears, contains language which may
be interpreted in two very different ways; and which might quite
conceivably have been <u>intended</u> as a double-entendre calling both
interpretations to mind. The two interpretations are reflected
by the two drastically different ways in which major parts of
the section may be <u>translated</u>! I offer this (extremely literal)
translation of 20b-29, reflecting the first of the two possible
interpretations.

> The ones who it is not given them to sin, the world (κόσμος)
> calls them "free" (ἐλεύθερος). These who it is not given to
> them to sin, the knowledge (γνῶσις) of the truth (ἀλήθεια)
> ["ⲧⲅⲛⲱⲥⲓⲥⲛ̄ⲧⲁⲗⲏⲑⲉⲓⲁ"] exalts. That is, it makes them free
> (ἐλεύθερος). And it exalts them over the whole place and
> (δέ) love (ἀγάπη) builds up;(10) and (δέ) the one who has

become free (ἐλεύθερος) by knowledge (γνῶσις) is a slave because of the love (ἀγάπη) for those whom not yet it has been given to be able to receive [the fr]eedom ([ἐ]λευθερία) of the knowledge (γνῶσις).(11)

The interpretation reflected by such a translation would take the first part of the section as basically a reiteration of what was said at 77,15b-18, a reiteration then probably followed by a fuller explication of the "way of life" -- "not sinning" -- resulting from the "freedom" associated with "the knowledge of the truth." The opening lines (20b-21) would be taken as simply a recapitulation, in reverse order, of the earlier statements that the ones who are "free" because of their "knowledge of the truth" do not sin. That is, in this case, the statement that "it is not given them to sin" precedes the statement concerning "freedom." These "free ones," again called those to whom "it is not given...them to sin," are then directly associated with "the knowledge of the truth"; and the consequences of that association are made clear. It results in their "exaltation"; it is explicitly stated that "the knowledge of the truth" makes them "free," a "freedom" also resulting in some sort of ultimate exaltation.

The remaining lines of the section would then be taken as depicting the positive characteristics of the "way of life" associated with "the knowledge of the truth," a "way of life" previously described negatively -- as "not sinning." "Love" becomes a factor. These "free" ones are actually "slaves," but slaves of "love" -- not of "sin."(12) A very skillful writer would thus appear to be responsible for these lines. That is, it was initially stated (77,15b-18) that "the knowledge of the truth" makes one "free," so that he can not be a "slave of sin." "Freedom" is then again associated with "the knowledge of the truth"(77,24-25). It is, however, next said that this "free" one is, in fact (paradoxically), actually a "slave" -- but the "slave" of "love," not "sin"! It is also specifically stated, a point of special relevance in light of the teaching of "section A" of Thom. Cont., that this slavery of "love" is directed toward those who have not yet received the freedom which knowledge gives -- that is, those who are still "blind men."

The term "ⲧⲅⲛⲱⲥⲓⲥⲛ̄ⲧⲁⲗⲏⲑⲉⲓⲁ," according to this first interpretation of the passage in question, would also seem to be -- as a technical term -- formally synonymous with "ἐπίγνωσις ἀληθείας" and "ⲡⲥⲟⲟⲩⲛⲛ̄ⲧⲙⲏⲉ." 1) If possession of "ⲧⲅⲛⲱⲥⲓⲥⲛ̄ⲧⲁⲗⲏⲑⲉⲓⲁ" makes one "free," "exalted," "exalted over the whole place," it surely is indicated that "being saved" is "intimately related" to the meaning of that phrase. 2) Since those who are associated with "ⲧⲅⲛⲱⲥⲓⲥⲛ̄ⲧⲁⲗⲏⲑⲉⲓⲁ" are designated as those to whom "it is not given to them to sin," and as those who become slaves of "love" to other men, it is also clearly indicated that "the knowledge of the truth" thus "necessarily expresses itself in one's way of life."(13) 3) As was the case with regard to "ⲧⲅⲛⲱⲥⲓⲥⲛ̄ⲧⲙⲉ," in this "Christian" text "the knowledge of the truth" -- in this case "ⲧⲅⲛⲱⲥⲓⲥⲛ̄ⲧⲁⲗⲏⲑⲉⲓⲁ" -- must represent, by definition: "correct Christian doctrine."

The second possible interpretation of 77,20b-29, which is quite different from the first, would take those lines as an indirect, <u>sarcastically framed</u> attempt to reinforce the "correct" meaning of "the knowledge of the truth" -- using in this case the term "ⲧⲅⲛⲱⲥⲓⲥⲛ̄ⲧⲁⲗⲏⲑⲉⲓⲁ" -- the correct meaning already stated at 77, 15-18 by use of the phrase "ⲧⲅⲛⲱⲥⲓⲥⲛ̄ⲧⲙⲉ." I have already indicated that this differing <u>interpretation</u> reflects the fact that major portions of those lines may -- and perhaps should -- be <u>translated differently</u> from the way previously suggested. Two factors might cause one to prefer this second translation of the passage, a <u>translation</u> which really suggests a different <u>meaning</u> for the Coptic than that suggested by the translation already presented. The expressions (at 77,20,22), translated literally as "it is not given to them to sin,"(14) might be legitimately taken as meaning: "They are not permitted to sin." Ménard and Till translate them in this way,(15) apparently taking "ⲥⲧⲟ" as the Coptic impersonal verbal form which translates "ἐνδέχομαι" (16) -- taken in <u>its</u> impersonal form meaning: "It is possible." (17) The passages in question would thus be translated: a) "The ones who can not possibly sin" (77,20); b) "These who can not possibly sin" (77,22). Secondly, the <u>usual</u> sense of the verbal idiom "ⲭⲓⲥⲉⲛ̄ϩⲏⲧ" (77,23), and a common meaning of the verb form "ⲭⲓⲥⲉ" (77,25), is <u>pejorative</u>. "Exalt" would thus be taken in the sense of "make arrogant," "make boastful."(18)

A third factor involved in the second interpretation of 77,20b-29, while not affecting the actual translation, vastly alters the real thrust of meaning of the term "world (κόσμος)" at 77, 21a. A survey of the uses of "ⲕⲟⲥⲙⲟⲥ" ("world") in Gos. Phil. shows that it often, if not indeed fundamentally, is also used <u>pejoratively</u>. That is, "the world" is often regarded as, and spoken of, as a place of deception and a realm of error and misapprehension.

Taking these factors into consideration, I offer this (less literal) translation of 77,20b-29, the <u>translation</u> reflecting the second of the two possible <u>interpretations</u> of that passage.

> The ones who can not possibly sin, the world (κόσμος) calls free (ἐλεύθερος). These who can not possibly sin, the knowledge (γνῶσις) of the truth (ἀλήθεια) makes arrogant. That is, it makes them free (ἐλεύθερος) and it causes them to become arrogant over everything. But (δέ) love (ἀγάπη) builds up and (δέ) the one who has become free (ἐλεύθερος) through knowledge (γνῶσις) is a slave because of love (ἀγάπη) for those who have not yet been able to receive [the fr]eedom ([ἐ]λευθερία) of knowledge (γνῶσις).

This second interpretation of 20b-29 demands three more prefatory remarks. 1) It suggests, as did the first interpretation, considerable literary sophistication on the part of the writer of Gos. Phil. 2) This interpretation, far from demanding the rejection of the analysis of "the knowledge of the truth" (as "ⲧⲅⲛⲱⲥⲓⲥⲛ̄ⲧⲙⲉ") derived from the explanation of 77,15-18 -- as has already been suggested -- may be taken as implicitly supporting that analysis. 3) The analysis suggesting this second interpretation demands the passage's division into two units: 77,20b-25a; 25b-29.

The exegesis of the first unit consists of four parts. 1) Those who can not possibly sin -- who are "not permitted to sin" -- who are not, therefore, really "free" at all, the illusion-prone "world" nevertheless calls "free."(77,20b-22a) 2) "The knowledge (γνῶσις) of the truth (ἀλήθεια)," represented from the erroneous point of view of "the world," actually makes these persons who are not really "free," and who as part of that "world" themselves misunderstand "the knowledge of the truth," arrogant and presumptuous!(77,22b-23) 3) "That is, it makes them free (ἐλεύθερος)" -- "free" in the sense of arrogant licentiousness! (77,24) 4) The arrogant "freedom" of these persons, so wrongly called "free," even makes them feel "superior to" everything in creation!(77,25b)

These lines would thus be taken as a statement of how those who are not really free also represent the total misunderstanding of the real meaning -- already outlined at 77,15-18 -- of "the knowledge of the truth." This misunderstanding, of course, reflects the total misapprehension, by "the world," of the real nature of both "freedom" and (naturally) of: "the knowledge of the truth." This total misunderstanding of "the knowledge of the truth" is also, obviously, reflected in a total misapprehension of the attitude and conduct ("way of life") which would be "expressed" by one really "understanding" "the knowledge of the truth." That "arrogant" misunderstanding is, however, depicted in a context which will allow it to be contrasted with -- "corrected by" -- the depiction, in the second part of the section (77,25b-29), of the "way of life" of those who are really free.

"But (δέ)" -- in contrast to arrogant licentiousness -- "love (ἀγάπη) builds up and (δέ) the one who has [really] become free (ἐλεύθερος) through knowledge (γνῶσις) is [in fact] a slave because of love (ἀγάπη) for those who have not yet been able to receive [the fr]eedom ([ἐ]λευθερία) of knowledge (γνῶσις)."(25b-29a) 77,25-26a is clearly based on 1 Cor. 8:1. The wording in the Sahidic Coptic version is: "ⲡⲥⲟⲟⲩⲛ [Greek "γνῶσις"] ϣⲁϥϫⲓⲥⲉ ["puffs up"] ⲧⲁⲅⲁⲡⲏ ⲇⲉ ϣⲁⲥⲕⲱⲧ" ["but (δέ) love (ἀγάπη) builds up"]. The "way of life" of one set free by gnosis -- probably only a restatement of the authentic freedom indicated just a few lines earlier in the statement involving "the knowledge (γνῶσις) of the truth ["ⲧⲅⲛⲱⲥⲓⲥⲛ̄ⲧⲙⲉ"]" -- (19) consists of a "freedom" which is in fact a slavery compelled by "love," not the slavery to sin rejected at 77,15-18. It could thus be argued that "the

knowledge of the truth" described accurately at 77,15-18, and
the conduct it was said to produce ("not sinning"), are iron-
ically contrasted here with a false understanding of "the knowledge of the truth" and the arrogant, licentious conduct produced
by that false understanding -- a conduct then "corrected," however, by a statement affirming the authentic Christian conduct
of a life of love. This second interpretation would also suggest, moreover, that this "correction" of that "conduct" is actually meant to represent a "correction" of all of "the world"'s
"false understandings" -- including that of "the knowledge of
the truth" -- as that particular "misunderstanding" has been so
sarcastically characterized at 77,20b-25a. The actual arrogant
conduct "corrected" is, of course, only the final logical consequence of the totality of "the world"'s delusions described
there.

This second interpretation would take this passage as a sarcastic, typically Gnostic, polemic against "the world" which mis-
understands the real nature of "freedom," "the knowledge of the
truth," and the "way of life" related to that "knowledge." The
purpose of that polemic, however, would be to contrast that misunderstanding with a true "understanding" of those matters and
thus to "correct" the view held by "the world." This argument
would, therefore, reinforce, by the method of sarcastically i-
ronic contrast, the real meaning -- already stated at 77,15-18
-- of "the knowledge of the truth." In such a sarcastic context
of double-entendre one would need not be surprised to find such
apparent logical inconsistencies as that inherent in the statements that those "who can not possibly sin" do, in fact, "sin"
-- by becoming arrogant.

One might, therefore, suggest that in this logion of Gos. Phil.
an extremely skillful writer has -- at 77,15-18 -- set forth the
real meaning of "the knowledge (γνῶσις) of the truth" as a technical term ("ⲧⲅⲛⲱⲥⲓⲥⲛ̄ⲧⲙⲏⲉ") having the same formally-defined facets of technical meaning represented by both "ⲡⲥⲟⲟⲩⲛⲛ̄ⲧⲙⲏⲉ" and
"ἐπίγνωσις ἀληθείας." He has then, later in the logion, reit-
erated the meaning of "the knowledge of the truth" as a technical term by a complex argument revolving about the phrase "the
knowledge (γνῶσις) of the truth (ἀλήθεια)" -- expressed by the
Coptic term "ⲧⲅⲛⲱⲥⲓⲥⲛ̄ⲧⲁⲗⲏⲑⲉⲓⲁ." This "complex" argument, one
could well suggest, is really a double argument, both aspects of
which were meant to be called simultaneously to the mind of the
reader - a total double-entendre. One of them (the "first interpretation") continues the argument at 77,15-18 in a rather
straightforward manner; and clearly identifies that term with
all of the formally-defined aspects of the technical meaning of
"ⲡⲥⲟⲟⲩⲛⲛ̄ⲧⲙⲏⲉ" and "ἐπίγνωσις ἀληθείας." The other (the "second
interpretation") indirectly, and quite subtly, supports the real
meaning of "the knowledge of the truth" by sarcastically contrasting the mistaken view held by "the world" of the meaning of
that term, and matters related to it, with the real meanings in
question. This complex argument -- if it is a correct inter-

pretation -- joined to the argument derived from 77,15-18 regarding "ⲧⲅⲛⲱⲥⲓⲥⲛ̄ⲧⲙⲉ," would provide the strongest argument for suggesting that "ⲧⲅⲛⲱⲥⲓⲥⲛ̄ⲧⲙⲉ" and "ⲧⲅⲛⲱⲥⲓⲥⲛ̄ⲧⲁⲗⲏⲑⲓⲁ" function together in logion 110 of Gos. Phil. to establish "the knowledge of the truth" as a technical term there formally synonymous with both "ⲡⲥⲟⲟⲩⲛⲛ̄ⲧⲙⲏⲉ" and "ἐπίγνωσις ἀληθείας."

The argument in which one must ultimately become involved, before coming to any final conclusion as to the possible relevance of this logion in Gos. Phil. to the overall purpose of this investigation, is -- unfortunately but necessarily -- of extreme complexity. It seems advisable at this point, therefore, both to recapitulate briefly what has already been said about this logion and to present a brief preparatory outline of the argument which will then follow.

It should be quite clear, from what has already been said, that there are numerous reasons compelling the consideration of these two Coptic terms in Gos. Phil. as part of the historical survey seeking possible parallels to the technical terms "ⲡⲥⲟⲟⲩⲛⲛ̄ⲧⲙⲏⲉ" and "ἐπίγνωσις ἀληθείας." 1) A quite straightforward argument can be made that "ⲧⲅⲛⲱⲥⲓⲥⲛ̄ⲧⲙⲉ" ("the knowledge of the truth") at CG II:77,16 (in the context of 77,15-18) should be taken as a technical term which is, formally-defined, synonymous with the purely formal definitions of both "ⲡⲥⲟⲟⲩⲛⲛ̄ⲧⲙⲏⲉ" and "ἐπίγνωσις ἀληθείας." 2) I believe I have shown that it is possible that an equally straightforward argument can be made to suggest that "ⲧⲅⲛⲱⲥⲓⲥⲛ̄ⲧⲁⲗⲏⲑⲓⲁ" ("the knowledge of the truth") at 77,23 might serve as another synonymous (formally-defined) technical term reinforcing the meaning of "ⲧⲅⲛⲱⲥⲓⲥⲛ̄ⲧⲙⲉ" at 77,16. 3) I have outlined a second interpretation of 77,20-29 which, in a quite different and far more complex way, would suggest the same conclusion regarding the function of "ⲧⲅⲛⲱⲥⲓⲥⲛ̄ⲧⲁⲗⲏⲑⲓⲁ" as a technical term. 4) I have suggested that it is possible that those two interpretations of 77,20-29 might have been both intended to be called to the reader's mind, intimating a double-entendre argument meant to reinforce the meaning of "ⲧⲅⲛⲱⲥⲓⲥⲛ̄ⲧⲙⲉ" at 77,16 as a technical term. 5) Finally, I have pointed out that the strongest possible argument that the two Coptic terms function together to establish "the knowledge of the truth" as an emphatic technical term in Gos. Phil. would consist of a combination of the straightforward argument regarding "ⲧⲅⲛⲱⲥⲓⲥⲛ̄ⲧⲙⲉ" derived from the analysis of 77,15-18 and the double-entendre argument regarding "ⲧⲅⲛⲱⲥⲓⲥⲛ̄ⲧⲁⲗⲏⲑⲓⲁ" derived from analysis of 77,20-29. It should, therefore, be obvious why I have had to take logion 110 of Gos. Phil. into serious consideration as a necessary part of this study.

I must, in all honesty however, also outline the arguments which could -- sometimes quite legitimately -- be raised against each of the arguments just presented. That is, it could be argued that there is no technical term meaning "the knowledge of the truth" in logion 110 of Gos. Phil.! Nevertheless, I must also then explain the reasons indicating that it would be irresponsible for me -- in light of the purpose of this study -- to dismiss the real possibility that there is <u>at least one</u> technical term for "the knowledge of the truth," which is formally synonymous with "ⲡⲥⲟⲟⲩⲛ̄ⲧⲙⲏⲉ" and "ἐπίγνωσις ἀληθείας," in this part of <u>Gos. Phil</u>. At that point it will, therefore, be necessary to consider what would constitute the "content definition" of such a technical term for "Christsein" derived from the "basic teaching" of <u>Gos. Phil</u>.

I must now turn to the various objections which could be raised against my arguments for the existence of a technical term -- "the knowledge of the truth" -- in logion 110 of <u>Gos. Phil</u>.

1) The, so very complex, double-entendre argument regarding the term "ⲧⲅⲛⲱⲥⲓⲥⲛ̄ⲧⲁⲗⲏⲑⲉⲓⲁ" derived from 77,20-29 -- basically involving 77,20-25 -- can certainly be seriously questioned. Does it not appear to presuppose a writer of almost incredible skill and subtlety? The two <u>translations</u> of the Coptic required by the two <u>interpretations</u> (leaving aside the fact that the Coptic presumably represents translation of a lost Greek <u>Vorlage</u>) actually almost give the impression that they are translations of <u>different Coptic texts</u>.(20) The two interpretations reflected in those translations are, moreover, <u>so</u> different! Even if one assumes a writer capable of such language, is it really likely that he would expect his readers to grasp such a <u>radical</u> double-entendre? More specifically, would a writer use <u>the Vorlagen</u> of "ⲥⲧⲟ," "ⲭⲓⲥⲉⲛ̄ϩⲏⲧ," "ⲭⲓⲥⲉ" -- and the word "κόσμος" -- expecting each of the terms to be interpreted simultaneously in two such radically different ways? The extreme double-entendre argument for the interpretation of 77,20-25 seems, although possible, actually <u>quite</u> strained!

If it is agreed that such a double interpretation of those lines is strained, one must choose between the two. In that case, the meanings of "ⲥⲧⲟ," "ⲭⲓⲥⲉⲛ̄ϩⲏⲧ," (especially) "ⲭⲓⲥⲉ" and "ⲕⲟⲥⲙⲟⲥ" which form the basis of the "second interpretation" of 77,20-25 would seem -- for the reasons already cited -- to make it the more likely of the two. If one accepts that option, however, other problems then appear. <u>Gos. Phil</u>., a "Christian" text, has apparently already given one <u>interpretation</u> of the meaning of "the knowledge of the truth" ("ⲧⲅⲛⲱⲥⲓⲥⲛ̄ⲧⲙⲉ") as a technical term representing "Christsein" -- in this same logion at 77,15-18. There it was said that "the knowledge of the truth" makes one free, that is, he does <u>not</u> sin. Furthermore, the passage now in question (20b-25) is immediately followed by the statement at 77,26-29 (probably echoing 1 Cor. 8:1) that the Christian virtue of "ἀγάπη" "builds up"; and also by the statement that the free one becomes a "slave" of "love" for other men who are not yet "free." Considering this preceding and following context, even if the words at 77,20b-25 were <u>meant</u> to be taken sarcastically, would not the average reader be surprised -- and/or offended -- by statements that: "the knowledge of the truth" makes one "ar-

rogant"; "arrogant over everything"; and <u>licentiously</u> "free"?
If the two Coptic terms for "the knowledge of the truth" in this
logion were <u>really</u> meant to represent the <u>same</u> view of "Christsein," does it not seem that a real problem would be presented
for any ordinary reader by the two, at least <u>apparently</u>, quite
opposed definitions of them which the "second interpretation" of
77,20b-29 would demand?

The "second interpretation" of 77,20b-29 also presents another
problem, one it shares with the "first interpretation" of those
lines. That common problem is, however, especially critical to
the second interpretation. It has been pointed out that it is
not absolutely certain that the slavery to "love" of the one who
has been made "free" by "ⲅⲛⲱⲥⲓⲥ" is also to be associated with
the "freedom" of the one made "free" by "ⲧⲅⲛⲱⲥⲓⲥⲛ̄ⲧⲁⲗⲏⲑⲉⲓⲁ."(21)
This "association" is <u>essential</u> to the second interpretation because the crucial element in the entire "correction" of the erroneous view held by "the world" of the matters in question consists of contrasting its view of the "way of life" related to
"the knowledge of the truth" with "love" -- "love" as the <u>real</u>
expression of the Christian "way of life" "the [real] knowledge
of the truth" represents. I discussed the "mother-father" language at 77,19-20a precisely because, not only here but also at
77,16, it would be helpful if that language did indeed indicate
that the technical term(s) in question always consist(s) of a
<u>combination</u> of "the knowledge" and "the truth." If that should
<u>be the case</u>, at 77,26-27 where only "ⲅⲛⲱⲥⲓⲥ" appears, that term
simply would be taken as "shorthand" for the compound technical
term -- "the knowledge <u>of the truth</u>" -- which then is really always meant to be taken <u>as the</u> "agent" of "freedom" and which is
also correctly understood when expressed by "love."

The argument about the possible meaning of the "mother-father"
language, as was just noted, does also speak to the (possible)
necessary unity of the two nouns in the phrase "ⲧⲅⲛⲱⲥⲓⲥⲛ̄ⲧⲙⲉ" at
77,16 and to the analysis of <u>that</u> phrase as a technical term, an
analysis which has seemed quite straightforward and unquestion-
able up to this point. The possible problem in the analysis of
"ⲧⲅⲛⲱⲥⲓⲥⲛ̄ⲧⲙⲉ" to which the "two-parent" argument would speak is
caused by the fact that there appears to be evidence throughout
<u>Gos. Phil.</u> that both "knowledge" ("ⲅⲛⲱⲥⲓⲥ") and "truth" ("ⲙⲉ" or
"ⲁⲗⲏⲑⲉⲓⲁ") can stand <u>alone</u> as technical terms seeming to have
much the same meaning suggested for the compound technical term,
"the knowledge of the truth." If this is the case, the entire
analysis of "ⲧⲅⲛⲱⲥⲓⲥⲛ̄ⲧⲙⲉ" as a technical term would also seem
possibly called into question.

It was pointed out during the initial examination of this text
that the use of "ⲙⲉ" at 77,16 might represent the apparent tendency, in Gos. Phil., to use "the truth" in a way which reflects
the Johannine technical usage of "ἀλήθεια." When, and if, "the
truth" ("ⲙⲉ," "ⲁⲗⲏⲑⲉⲓⲁ") is used technically in <u>Gos. Phil.</u> in
its Johannine sense, it would appear synonymous with the formal

definition of "the knowledge of the truth" as a technical term
in logion 110. It would appear self-evident that the technical
term "ἀλήθεια" in the Fourth Gospel, purely formally-defined,
represents "correct Christian doctrine" which "necessarily expresses
itself in one's way of life" and which is "intimately
related to 'being saved.'" In this logion "ⲙⲉ," therefore, or
"ⲁⲗⲏⲑⲉⲓⲁ" -- the term used in logion 123 already cited as being
paradigmatic of this Johannine use of "the truth" in Gos. Phil.
-- might actually be the technical term in question (at 77,16
and 77,23), not "the knowledge of the truth." The use of the
word "ⲅⲛⲱⲥⲓⲥ," in the phrase "the knowledge of the truth," then
might possibly simply reflect the obvious fact that Gos. Phil.
is a "Gnostic" text.

It could also be argued, in the exact reverse fashion, that in
logion 110 the real technical term in question is "ⲅⲛⲱⲥⲓⲥ," or
at least that it is synonymous with "the knowledge of the truth"
and could alone carry all the technical meaning associated with
that phrase. I have already pointed out the problem raised by
the question as to whether or not the slavery to "love" of the
one made "free" by "ⲅⲛⲱⲥⲓⲥ" (26b-28a) is a condition which might
exist independently from the freedom made possible by "ⲧⲅⲛⲱⲥⲓⲥ
ⲛ̄ⲧⲁⲗⲏⲑⲉⲓⲁ" (77,23-24). It could also be argued that the double
statement at 77,26-29 that "ⲧⲅⲛⲱⲥⲓⲥ" gives "[fr]eedom," or makes
one "free,"(22) might equate "ⲧⲅⲛⲱⲥⲓⲥ" with "ⲧⲅⲛⲱⲥⲓⲥⲛ̄ⲧⲙⲉ" (77,
16) which makes one "free." If "ⲧⲅⲛⲱⲥⲓⲥ" can make one "free,"
and a "slave" of "love" for others, it could then alone serve as
a formally-defined technical term which is "intimately related
to 'being saved'" which "necessarily expresses itself in one's
way of life." In a "Christian-Gnostic" text, like Gos. Phil.,
obviously "correct Christian doctrine" could be represented by
the term "ⲧⲅⲛⲱⲥⲓⲥ."(23)

My analysis must, therefore, take into account the strong individual
technical associations of, respectively, "ⲁⲗⲏⲑⲉⲓⲁ," "ⲙⲉ"
and "ⲅⲛⲱⲥⲓⲥ." It is for this reason that the section presenting
the "two-parent" argument is important. It quite possibly was
intended, in light of its connecting position between the sections
containing the two phrases meaning "the knowledge of the
truth," as a reminder that those compound terms -- despite the
technical associations of the three individual terms contained
in them -- were meant to be taken as the fundamental technical
terms of this logion. Without the "two-parent" argument, therefore,
one could suggest that even the phrase "ⲧⲅⲛⲱⲥⲓⲥⲛ̄ⲧⲙⲉ" is
not a technical term.

Despite the strength of many of these objections which can be
raised against my prior arguments, in light of the purposes of
this study, the arguments which can also be raised to counter
many of those objections are strong enough that I must -- as already
stated -- accept the real possibility that Gos. Phil. contains
at least one technical term meaning "the knowledge of the
truth" which is formally synonymous with both "ⲡⲥⲟⲟⲩⲛⲛ̄ⲧⲙⲏⲉ" and

"ἐπίγνωσις ἀληθείας." My final conclusion regarding the possible relevance of logion 110 of Gos. Phil. to the relationship between those same two technical terms must -- for the reasons now to be cited -- even take into account the possibility that "ⲧⲅⲛⲱⲥⲓⲥⲛ̄ⲧⲙⲉ" and "ⲧⲅⲛⲱⲥⲓⲥⲛ̄ⲧⲁⲗⲏⲉⲓⲁ" function as mutually reinforcing technical terms in Gos. Phil.

1) One could insist that it is not inconceivable that the logion does represent the work of an extremely sophisticated literary artist capable of intending(24) the double-entendre interpretation of 77,20-29 meant to fix "ⲧⲅⲛⲱⲥⲓⲥⲛ̄ⲧⲁⲗⲏⲉⲓⲁ" as a technical term reinforcing the meaning of the technical term "ⲧⲅⲛⲱⲥⲓⲥⲛ̄ⲧⲙⲉ" at 77,16. I am not personally so persuaded. Nevertheless, any final conclusion about the relevance of the logion to the purpose of this study can not ignore that possibility. 2) It is also possible -- actually much less inconceivable -- that the technical term "ⲧⲅⲛⲱⲥⲓⲥⲛ̄ⲧⲙⲉ" at 77,16 was meant to be reinforced by "ⲧⲅⲛⲱⲥⲓⲥⲛ̄ⲧⲁⲗⲏⲉⲓⲁ" interpreted in only one of the two ways suggested. In that case, for the linguistic reasons cited, the "second interpretation" appears the much more likely valid of the two.

I have pointed out two objections to, or problems in, that interpretation. It could be argued that neither of them is really insurmountable. 1) The apparent conflict between the meaning of "the knowledge of the truth" presented by "ⲧⲅⲛⲱⲥⲓⲥⲛ̄ⲧⲙⲉ" and that presented by the sarcastic interpretation of "ⲧⲅⲛⲱⲥⲓⲥⲛ̄ⲧⲁⲗⲏⲉⲓⲁ" -- as well as the conflict between that interpretation and the message in the following lines (26-29) -- would not necessarily have affected the reader as I suggested. The "sarcasm" of 77, 20-25 could have been taken precisely as that -- "sarcasm." The reader, in that case, would not necessarily have been confused or offended by the language of those lines. 2) The essential association of the slavery to "love," directly related only to freedom "through knowledge (γνῶσις)," with the freedom given by "ⲧⲅⲛⲱⲥⲓⲥⲛ̄ⲧⲁⲗⲏⲉⲓⲁ" is made possible, one could argue, for three reasons. A link between freedom and "ⲧⲅⲛⲱⲥⲓⲥⲛ̄ⲧⲁⲗⲏⲉⲓⲁ" was established in the prior context at 77,23-24. Freedom has been already directly associated with "the knowledge of the truth," represented by the term "ⲧⲅⲛⲱⲥⲓⲥⲛ̄ⲧⲙⲉ." The "two-parent" argument already discussed might indicate that "ⲧⲅⲛⲱⲥⲓⲥ" at 77,27 is just "shorthand" for "the knowledge of the truth" -- in this case "ⲧⲅⲛⲱⲥⲓⲥⲛ̄ⲧⲁⲗⲏⲉⲓⲁ."

For these reasons I will admit that it is conceivable that the term "ⲧⲅⲛⲱⲥⲓⲥⲛ̄ⲧⲁⲗⲏⲉⲓⲁ" at 77,23 may have been meant to function in a way which would reinforce the meaning of "ⲧⲅⲛⲱⲥⲓⲥⲛ̄ⲧⲙⲉ" at 77,16 -- thus establishing "the knowledge of the truth" as a most emphatic technical term having the same formal definition as both "ⲡⲥⲟⲟⲩⲛⲛ̄ⲧⲙⲏⲉ" and "ἐπίγνωσις ἀληθείας." Any final conclusion regarding the possible relevance of this logion to the overall question at hand must admit that such an analysis -- although in my view quite dubious -- is possible. I am, however, convinced that even if one ignores "ⲧⲅⲛⲱⲥⲓⲥⲛ̄ⲧⲁⲗⲏⲑⲉⲓⲁ," the probability that "ⲧⲅⲛⲱⲥⲓⲥⲛ̄ⲧⲙⲉ" is a technical term formally synonymous with "ⲡⲥⲟⲟⲩⲛⲛ̄ⲧⲙⲏⲉ" and "ἐπίγνωσις ἀληθείας" must be taken quite seriously! The reasons for suggesting this possibility were outlined at the beginning of this section of the discussion. Even given the individual technical associations of both "ⲅⲛⲱⲥⲓⲥ" and "ⲙⲉ" in Gos. Phil., in the context of 77,15-18 -- and taking into account the (in my opinion) quite probably valid "two-parent" argument -- the phrase "ⲧⲅⲛⲱⲥⲓⲥⲛ̄ⲧⲙⲉ" at 77,16 must be taken as a very possible representation of "Christsein" with the same three facets of technical meaning found in "ἐπίγνωσις ἀληθείας" and "ⲡⲥⲟⲟⲩⲛⲛ̄ⲧⲙⲏⲉ."

Even so, however, the "content definition" of "the knowledge of the truth" -- "Christsein" -- demanded by the "basic teaching" of Gos. Phil. would differ considerably, in particularly relevant ways, from the "content definition" of "the knowledge of the truth" ("Christsein") demanded by the "basic teaching" of "section A" of Thom. Cont. I must, therefore, offer here a survey of the key aspects of the "basic teaching" of Gos. Phil. -- as it is related to that of "section A" of Thom. Cont. I cite passages from Gos. Phil.(25) representative of each of the three aspects of the relationship I find between its "basic teaching" and that of "section A" of Thom. Cont. That is, I shall quote: 1) passages which show Gos. Phil. to be in basic agreement with "section A" of Thom. Cont.; 2) passages which show the teaching of Gos. Phil. to be much more complex, sophisticated and "orthodox" than that found in "section A" of Thom. Cont.; 3) passages which show aspects of the "basic teaching" of Gos. Phil. totally contrary to the "basic teaching" of "section A" of Thom. Cont.

One would expect to find basic areas of agreement between two "Christian-Gnostic" texts such as Gos. Phil. and Thom. Cont. I shall, therefore, treat here only the most critical aspect of their doctrinal agreement, the doctrinal element in Gos. Phil. which is most characteristic of, and crucial to, "section A" of Thom. Cont. There is considerable emphasis in Gos. Phil. upon the deprecation of "this world" and "the flesh," accompanied by expressions rejecting worldly "ἐπιθυμία" and affirming the need for "escape" from this body and (evil) world. I cite only two paradigmatic passages. "Fear not the flesh nor love it. If you fear it, it will gain mastery over you. If you love it, it will swallow and paralyze you."(26) "He who comes out of the world can no longer be detained, because he was in the world. It is evident that he is above desire ["ⲉⲡⲓⲑⲩⲙⲓⲁ"]...."(27)

The more complex and "orthodox" nature of the teaching of Gos. Phil., vis-à-vis the rather simplictic and almost totally "non-orthodox" teaching of "section A" of Thom. Cont., is quite significant in differentiating any definition of "Christsein" to be found in Gos. Phil. from that reflected in the "content definition" of "ⲡⲥⲟⲟⲩⲛⲛ̄ⲧⲙⲏⲉ." The first passage which may be cited to show this more complex and "orthodox" dimension of the teaching of Gos. Phil. also contains specific doctrines of particular relevance to this comparison. "Christ came to ransom some, to save others, to redeem others. He ransomed those who were strangers and made them his own....It was not only when he appeared that he voluntarily laid down his life, but he voluntarily laid down his life from the very day the world came into being."(28) The, at least apparent, differentiation between those "ransomed," those "saved" and those "redeemed" is certainly complex and -- admittedly -- not to be found in the Bible. Similarly, the idea that Christ "laid down his life" -- "not only when he appeared...but...from the very day the world came into being" -- is quite complex and non-Biblical. This passage, however, differentiates the teaching of Gos. Phil. from that found in "section A" of Thom. Cont. in far more important ways than by merely showing that Gos. Phil. contains a much more complex type of teaching. Although the ideas are expressed in a quite aberrant way -- and in a context which contains totally non-Biblical teachings -- the passage does still affirm the "orthodox" ideas that Christ's mission involved "ransom" and "redeeming," doctrines totally foreign to Thom. Cont. and central to the Pastorals. According to this passage in Gos. Phil., that mission thus also involved the crucifixion ("laid down his life") -- never mentioned even indirectly in Thom. Cont. Gos. Phil. even contains, elsewhere, the phrase: "the power of the cross."(29)

The next passage to be cited, besides describing a very complex teaching, also indicates that another important "orthodox" doctrine -- totally lacking in "section A" of Thom. Cont. -- is important to the doctrine of Gos. Phil. "'The Father' and 'the Son' are single names, 'the Holy Spirit' is a double name."(30) The "Holy Spirit" is specifically mentioned. It is even conceivable that some sort of "Trinitarian" assertion is intended. Any doctrine of the "Holy Spirit," let alone of the "Trinity," is obviously totally alien to Thom. Cont. This passage is, of course, just one of many in Gos. Phil. which refer to the "Holy Spirit."

The final passage I quote as indicating the complexity of the teaching of Gos. Phil. also shows the importance that text attaches to "orthodox" Christian "virtues" which are clearly irrelevant to the "basic teaching" of "section A" of Thom. Cont. "Faith receives, love gives. [No one will be able to receive] without faith. No one will be able to give without love. Because of this, in order that we may indeed receive, we believe, but it is so that we may love and give, since if one does not give in love, he has no profit from what is given."(31) "Faith" and "belief" are foreign to "section A" of Thom. Cont. -- as is any positive ethic! It is clear, from the citation of just this passage, that a positive ethic -- "love" -- is important to the "basic teaching" of Gos. Phil.(32)

The point in question has surely been adequately demonstrated.

Although the "basic teachings" of "section A" of Thom. Cont. and Gos. Phil. share (naturally) some "Gnostic" tenets, the doctrine of "section A" of Thom. Cont. is sharply differentiated from the doctrine of Gos. Phil. in that the latter text contains a much more complex and "orthodox" "basic teaching" than is to be found in Thom. Cont.

This differentiation between the two "basic teachings" in question is reflected even more dramatically by the fact that there are numerous statements in Gos. Phil. representing ideas -- or "ways of thinking" -- directly contrary to the "basic teaching" of "section A" of Thom. Cont. I shall again cite a few of the most striking representative examples. Much has been written about the importance and possible meaning of the "bridal chamber" image in Gos. Phil., a complex problem which can, and need, not be reviewed here. It is a matter of significance for this study, however, that implicitly sexual imagery, even if it is interpreted in the most "spiritualized" way, plays an important role in the teaching of Gos. Phil. Even such a method of teaching (no matter how "spiritualized" in imagery) is inconceivable in either section of Thom. Cont., a compulsively, almost psychotically anti-sexual text!

The writer(s) of "section A" of Thom. Cont. would have been repelled by language such as: "For it is by a kiss that the perfect conceive and give birth. For this reason we also kiss one another. We receive conception from the grace which is in each other."(33) The "way of thinking" responsible for the "basic teaching" of "section A" of Thom. Cont. would reject the use of such language -- no matter what idea those words were meant to convey! Another passage from Gos. Phil. shows even more clearly that the compulsive anti-sexuality -- so "basic" to the "basic teaching" of Thom. Cont. -- is not shared by Gos. Phil.(34) It is stated, in Gos. Phil., that: "Surely what a man accomplishes depends on his abilities. We...refer to one's accomplishments as 'abilities.' Among his accomplishments are his children." (35) In the view of "section A" of Thom. Cont. the fact that men "beget" (children) is almost paradigmatic of the "problem" of human existence!

I quote one additional "bridal chamber" passage from Gos. Phil., one which both reinforces this point and also provides an ideal transition to the demonstration of the next point of differentiation between the "basic teachings" of Gos. Phil. and "section A" of Thom. Cont. "A bridal chamber is not for the animals, nor is it for the slaves, nor for the defiled women; but it is for the free men and the virgins."(36) In addition to the fact that even such imagery would be unthinkable in Thom. Cont., in "section A" man's "problem" is often depicted by use of the motif of "bestiality,"(37) his likeness to other "animals." The crucial aspect of this likeness, furthermore, consists of the fact that both men and the other animals indulge in sexual activity. Gos. Phil., however, actually uses sexual imagery in order to -- among other things -- <u>differentiate men from animals</u>! "A bridal chamber is not for the animals...but it is for the free men and the virgins."

This difference of opinion on the relationship between men and the animals is a quite important point of contrast between the "basic teaching" of <u>Gos. Phil.</u> and that of "section A" of <u>Thom. Cont.</u> As was just pointed out, mankind's likeness to the <u>other animals</u> is viewed as a fundamental representation of his basic problem in "section A." I quote here just one of several passages in <u>Gos. Phil.</u> which stresses the great differentiation between men and other creatures ("beasts").

> <u>The superiority of man is not obvious to the eye</u>, but lies in what is hidden from view. Consequently <u>he has mastery over the animals which are stronger than he</u> is and great <u>in terms of the obvious</u> and the hidden. This enables them to survive. But if man is separated from them, they slay one another and bite one another. They ate one another <u>because they did not find any food. But now they have food because man tilled the soil</u>.(38)

This passage in <u>Gos. Phil.</u> unequivocally asserts men's superiority over -- let alone differentiation from -- the animals. It even stresses the animals' dependence upon men.

These lines also represent one of the most blatant examples of a phenomenon noted in the previous section, the fact that the thought found in <u>Gos. Phil.</u> is much more sophisticated (complex) than the rather simplictic thought found in "section A" of <u>Thom. Cont.</u> In <u>Gos. Phil.</u> it is here said that, <u>on the surface</u>, the <u>superiority</u> of men over the animals is not apparent -- exactly the point of view on the relationship between men and the other "beasts" found in "section A" of <u>Thom. Cont.</u> <u>Gos. Phil.</u>, however, then immediately states that <u>if one looks beyond</u> the superficial appearances, a vastly different picture is presented. The thinking reflected in "section A" of <u>Thom. Cont.</u> does not take this additional step to look beyond the superficial -- especially sexual -- similarities between men and the beasts of the field.

It should now be quite clear that, despite certain affinities, <u>very</u> significant differences exist between the "basic teaching" of <u>Gos. Phil.</u> and that of "section A" of <u>Thom. Cont.</u> If, therefore, logion 110 of <u>Gos. Phil.</u> does indeed contain "the knowledge of the truth" as a technical term which is formally synonymous with "ἐπίγνωσις ἀληθείας" and "ⲡⲥⲟⲟⲩⲛ ⲛ̄ⲧⲙⲏⲉ" as representations of "Christsein," the "content definition" of that term -- "the knowledge of the truth" as "Christsein" -- demanded by the "basic teaching" of <u>Gos. Phil.</u> would certainly differ from that of "ⲡⲥⲟⲟⲩⲛ ⲛ̄ⲧⲙⲏⲉ" ("<u>Christsein</u>") which is demanded by the "basic teaching" of "section A" of <u>Thom. Cont.</u> Every aspect of that "content definition" of "ⲡⲥⲟⲟⲩⲛ ⲛ̄ⲧⲙⲏⲉ," as "Christsein," is diametrically opposed to the corresponding aspect of the ("orthodox") "content definition" of "ἐπίγνωσις ἀληθείας," as the version of "Christsein" demanded by the "basic teaching" of the Pastorals. It should be evident, from what has just been said about the "basic teaching" of Gos. Phil., that the same situation would not exist if one made a comparison between the "content definition" of "ἐπίγνωσις ἀληθείας" -- as "Christsein" -- and the "content definition" of any technical term in Gos. Phil. representing its version of "Christsein."

The third Coptic phrase in the Nag Hammadi corpus which demands thorough examination as part of this historical survey is found in The Apocalypse of Adam (CG V,5).(39) "ⲟⲩⲅⲛⲱⲥⲓⲥ ⲛ̄[ⲧⲉ]ⲧⲙⲉ," "knowledge (γνῶσις) o[f] the truth," appears in Apoc. Adam at CG V: 83,13b-14a. That phrase demands investigation here because it might well appear that, in its immediate context, "ⲟⲩⲅⲛⲱⲥⲓⲥ ⲛ̄[ⲧⲉ]ⲧⲙⲉ" could also function as a technical term having exactly the same formally-defined aspects of meaning as "ⲡⲥⲟⲟⲩⲛ̄ⲛ̄ⲧⲙⲏⲉ" and "ἐπίγνωσις ἀληθείας." The section, in the context of which the term in question must be interpreted, consists of CG V: 83, 8b-23a.

> Then (τότε) the peoples (λάος) will cry o[u]t with a great voice, saying: "Blessed is the soul (ψυχή) of those men because they have known God in a knowledge (γνῶσις) o[f] the truth. They will live for[e]ver (αἰ[ώ]ν; αἰών) because they have not been corrupted by their desire (ἐπιθυμία) together with the angels (ἄγγελος), nor (οὔτε) have they completed the works of the powers. Rather (ἀλλά) they have stood in his presence in a knowledge (γνῶσις) of God like light which has come out from fire and blood."(40)

1) It is thus said that the object of this "knowledge (γνῶσις) o[f] the truth" is "God" -- surely the Ultimate Subject of "correct Christian doctrine." 2) The "understanding" represented by "ⲟⲩⲅⲛⲱⲥⲓⲥ ⲛ̄[ⲧⲉ]ⲧⲙⲉ" would appear, for two reasons, to be quite "intimately related to 'being saved.'" "'Blessed is the soul (ψυχή) of those men because [emphasis added] they have known God in a knowledge (γνῶσις) o[f] the truth.'" There thus appears to be a causal relationship between "knowledge (γνῶσις) o[f] the truth" and possession of a "blessed...soul (ψυχή)," that is, a "saved" soul. These same men who "have known God in a knowledge (γνῶσις) o[f] the truth...will live for[e]ver (αἰ[ώ]ν; αἰών)." "Eternal life" may, of course, serve as a functional synonym for "salvation," "being saved." 3) It is then said that these men "have not been corrupted by their desire (ἐπιθυμία)...nor (οὔτε) have they completed the works of the powers." The language thus appears to associate a "way of life" with "ⲟⲩⲅⲛⲱⲥⲓⲥⲛ̄[ⲧⲉ]ⲧⲙⲉ," a "way of life" which consists of: a) noncorruption by "ἐπιθυμία"; b) not completing "the works of the [evil] powers." It should be clear that "ⲟⲩⲅⲛⲱⲥⲓⲥⲛ̄[ⲧⲉ]ⲧⲙⲉ" initially appears to function as a term formally synonymous with "ⲡⲥⲟⲟⲩⲛ̄ⲛ̄ⲧⲙⲏⲉ" and "ἐπίγνωσις ἀληθείας," thus being a term which must be considered as a part

of this study.

There are, however, reasons suggested, <u>even by that same immediate context</u> in which the phrase appears, for questioning whether "ⲟⲩⲅⲛⲱⲥⲓⲥⲛ̄[ⲧⲉ]ⲧⲙⲉ" really does serve in <u>Apoc. Adam</u> as a technical term with the formal definition initially indicated. G. W. MacRae has written, in one of his introductions to <u>Apoc. Adam</u>: "But in the end...those who have truly known the living God will live forever."(41) With those words in mind, one sees two possible indications in the passage in question that what is really being spoken of (what "saves," etc.) is not basically described by the phrase: "knowledge (γνῶσις) o[f] the truth." The matter of real importance could, rather, actually be called: "knowing God." Perhaps the language at 83,11-14 should be taken in this manner: "'Blessed is the soul (ψυχή) of those men <u>because they have known God</u> [emphasis added] in a knowledge (γνῶσις) o[f] the truth.'" The crucial point may be that "those men" are called "Blessed" "because they have known God." The importance of the phrase, "in a knowledge (γνῶσις) o[f] the truth," may be quite secondary to that of the words preceding it!

Such an interpretation is supported by the <u>total</u> description of "those men" as ones who: "...have not been corrupted by their desire (ἐπιθυμία)...nor (οὔτε) have they completed the works of the powers. Rather (ἀλλά) they have stood in his presence <u>in a knowledge (γνῶσις) of God</u> [emphasis added] like light...." To "have known God," or to have "a knowledge (γνῶσις) of God," may be the phrases of real importance -- in mere service of which "knowledge (γνῶσις) o[f] the truth" functions. That is, "knowledge (γνῶσις) o[f] the truth" may not be the really important terminology in this passage in <u>Apoc. Adam</u> at all.

There is a second, possibly more problematic, reason -- derived from the immediate context -- for questioning whether "knowledge (γνῶσις) o[f] the truth" in <u>Apoc. Adam</u> is a technical term of the type suggested. It is not at all certain that having known God "in a knowledge (γνῶσις) o[f] the truth" <u>causes</u> ("necessarily expresses itself in") the "way of life" involving rejection of "ἐπιθυμία," etc. It may actually be indicated (at 83,14b-19a) that the "way of life" in question is not really viewed as a "necessary expression" of having grasped "knowledge (γνῶσις) o[f] the truth" and the "salvation" ("blessedness") related to it. That "way of life" could also be interpreted as being the <u>cause</u> of "salvation" -- described in terms of "eternal life." "They will live for[e]ver (αἰ[ώ]ν; αἰών) <u>because</u> they have not been corrupted by their desire (ἐπιθυμία)....[emphasis added]" It is <u>possible</u>, of course, that the "way of life" in question could have been thought of as being both the "result" of having known God "in a knowledge (γνῶσις) o[f] the truth" -- being part of the expression of the resulting "salvation" -- and simultaneously being the reason for that "salvation," described in terms of "eternal life." In any case, however, it should be apparent that the immediate context alone provides reasons to question the argument that "ⲟⲩⲅⲛⲱⲥⲓⲥⲛ̄[ⲧⲉ]ⲧⲙⲉ" in <u>Apoc. Adam</u> functions as a technical term formally synonymous with "ἐπίγνωσις ἀληθείας" and "ⲡⲥⲟⲟⲩⲛⲛ̄ⲧⲙⲏⲉ."

Even if one accepts the initial argument that "ⲟⲩⲅⲛⲱⲥⲓⲥⲛ̄[ⲧⲉ]ⲧⲙⲉ" does serve as an emphatic technical term in <u>Apoc. Adam</u>, there is still a <u>fundamental</u> reason -- not dependent upon the admittedly ambiguously worded context in which that phrase appears -- an absolutely fundamental reason the phrase can not be accepted as being even <u>formally</u> synonymous with either "ἐπίγνωσις ἀληθείας" or "ⲡⲥⲟⲟⲩⲛⲛ̄ⲧⲙⲏⲉ"! Those two terms represent an "understanding" which: a) is of "correct <u>Christian</u> doctrine"; b) "necessarily expresses itself in one's ["Christian"] way of life"; c) is "intimately related to...the whole matter of ["Christian"] 'soteriology.'" Both terms thus represent (as "<u>Christsein</u>"): "everything involved in 'being <u>Christian</u>'"! These definitions have been restated in order to remind the reader that, no matter how aberrant or "heterodox" the "content" of the "doctrine" in <u>Thom. Cont.</u> may appear -- as I had to stress initially -- its writers considered themselves to be "Christians" and their "doctrine" to be the authentic version of "Christian doctrine." On the other hand, the only conclusion to be drawn from the various detailed analyses of <u>Apoc. Adam</u> is that its writer(s) did <u>not</u> consider himself (themselves) "Christian" and its "doctrine" as the authentic version of "Christian doctrine"!

As long ago as 1965 MacRae suggested that <u>Apoc. Adam</u> "appears to contain no reference whatever that can unmistakably be called Christian."(42) He found this phenomenon especially significant because:

> Gnosticism is essentially syncretistic; it does not seek to dissociate itself from other religions but to adopt elements of them and "purify" them. Virtually all the Gnostic literature known to us [in 1965] openly betrays its attempt to absorb traces of Christianity by deliberately mentioning at least some Christian personality as a true Gnostic.(43)

Much more recently MacRae has written, similarly: "Most interestingly, the <u>Apocalypse of Adam</u> does not disclose any explicitly Christian themes."(44) In his fullest discussion of <u>Apoc. Adam</u> he states: "What makes 'The Apocalypse of Adam' controversial is the fact that it contains no unmistakably Christian allusions, and the...revealer figure is at least not clearly portrayed as Christ."(45) MacRae's words "unmistakably,"(46) "not clearly,"(47) and "explicitly"(48) in the passages just cited might seem to indicate his reluctance to state unequivocally the totally "non-Christian" character of <u>Apoc. Adam</u>. The same type of reluctance might seem present in his statement: "The most notable feature of this work is the absence of any <u>explicit</u> or <u>clear</u> borrowings from the Christian tradition."(49)

The <u>basic</u> viewpoint represented in Macrae's two fullest discussions of the text makes it quite clear, however, that he <u>does</u>, in fact, unequivocally consider <u>Apoc. Adam</u> totally "non-Christian." He includes <u>Apoc. Adam</u> in <u>his list</u> of Nag Hammadi texts from which: "The case for <u>non-Christian Gnosticism in the collection</u> as a whole can be made...."(50) An unequivocal view of the non-Christian nature of <u>Apoc. Adam</u> is clearly reflected in his discussion -- in the same article -- of the relationship between <u>Apoc. Adam</u> and <u>The Gospel of the Egyptians</u> (CG III,2 and IV,2).

> "The Gospel of the Egyptians" portrays Seth himself as the Gnostic heavenly redeemer who in his final coming <u>is explicitly identified with Christ. This work is clearly a product of Christian Gnosticism</u>, but a close analysis of it <u>and a comparison with "The Apocalypse of Adam"</u> suggest that <u>here</u> we have another glimpse of the process by which <u>an originally non-Christian Gnostic myth</u> [reflected in <u>Apoc. Adam</u>] <u>was appropriated</u> and at least superficially christianized. (51)

The same unequivocal point of view is also reflected in his discussion there of a possible Gnostic background for "the theme of the deception of the powers" at 1 Cor. 2:6-8.(52) He suggests, as a possibly relevant Gnostic example of this "theme," CG V: 77, 4-20 where: "...the same theme occurs in 'The Apocalypse of Adam'...."(53) He then explicitly states that: "This example [in <u>Apoc. Adam</u>] too <u>is one that we encounter in a non-Christian Gnostic context</u>."(54)

MacRae has also characterized <u>Apoc. Adam</u> as possibly representing "a transitional stage in an evolution from Jewish to gnostic apocalyptic." His very brief consideration of that possibility gives no indication whatsoever that "Christianity" was involved in any way in such an "evolution."(55) He then again immediately relates <u>Apoc. Adam</u> to <u>The Gospel of the Egyptians</u> in a way which clearly indicates that <u>Apoc. Adam</u> is to be considered non-Christian. "Within the Nag Hammadi <u>collection</u> it [<u>Apoc. Adam</u>] has a great deal in common with <u>Gos. Eg.</u> (III,2) which seems to suppose <u>a christianized version of the story</u> [found in a non-Christian form in <u>Apoc. Adam</u>]."(56) It is thus clear that the most thorough analyst of this tractate, MacRae, considers it a totally non-Christian work.

In their early analysis of <u>Apoc. Adam</u> Böhlig and Labib considered it to be a probable witness to a "vorchristlicher Gnosis." (57) Their conclusion that the tractate is "<u>pre-Christian</u>" certainly need not be necessarily accepted today. Nevertheless, it is still relevant that Böhlig and Labib explicitly, <u>in several contexts</u>, rejected the view that "Christianity" is reflected in <u>Apoc. Adam</u>.(58)

Hedrick's very substantial study of <u>Apoc. Adam</u> must, finally, be taken into account with regard to the question of the "Christian" character of that text. The basic purpose of his work is a redaction analysis which, <u>per se</u>, would be irrelevant to this study. That redaction analysis, however, finds two originally totally separate "sources," the second of which itself consists of two separate sections, reflected in the present form of the text. His analysis also concluded that the religious orientation of the final redactor caused him to make other additions and changes in the text. This redaction outline, which MacRae apparently has accepted as a viable hypothesis,(59) thus demands that the "Christian" character of each of the sources -- and of the final redactor's work -- must be discussed individually. I shall briefly describe, therefore, the (my phrase) "Christian intent" of: "the A source"; each of the two sections of "the B source"; the final redactor.

Hedrick wrote of "the A source": "Source A is best described as a Jewish gnostic text."(60) The language of the section of his monograph devoted to "The Position of the Text ["the A source"] in the History of Religions"(61) indicates clearly that he still considers that "source" "Jewish gnostic" and, therefore, totally non-Christian. "The situation that best explains these phenomena in the text [its "characteristic religious ideas"] is the assumption that the text stands near the border between Jewish apocalypticism and Gnosticism."(62)

> Although the text draws heavily upon Jewish midrashic and apocalyptic traditions, there can be little question that it is gnostic. It does not stand on the border between Jewish apocalypticism and Gnosticism, but has already turned the corner into Gnosticism. Yet the emerging nature of that Gnosticism requires that it still use concepts and categories from Jewish traditions for expressing itself. The author (or his tradition) stood that close to...Jewish roots. The text stands on the gnostic side of the shift, and the trajectory of the shift is quite clearly from Jewish apocalypticism into Gnosticism.(63)

Absolutely nothing is said about any possible "Christian intent" in "the A section." The passage in <u>Apoc. Adam</u> containing the phrase in question ("ⲟⲩⲅⲛⲱⲥⲓⲥⲛ̄[ⲧⲉ]ⲧⲙⲉ") would be, according to Hedrick's redaction analysis, part of "the A section."(64)

Hedrick has also stated succinctly: "Source B appears to be a <u>non-Christian</u> gnostic text."(65) That statement certainly does represent a vastly "abstracted" formulation of the conclusions to be drawn from his full discussion of "The Character of the B Source."(66) He finds (as was indicated briefly above) two separate sections -- each of which may be <u>discussed</u> separately -- within that "source." "Two segments...remain of source B: the revelation of the three men and the episode of the illuminator. <u>The literary character and theology of these two segments will be discussed separately</u>."(67)

"The Revelation of the Three Men," according to Hedrick's outline, consists of the material at CG V: 65,24-66,12; 67,12-21. (68) I find no indication whatsoever, in his analysis, of any "Christian intent" which might underlie that section. The reader may consult Hedrick's full discussion for details.(69) One statement, indicative of Hedrick's view of the basic nature of the material in that section, may be quoted here. "The ideas in this revelation story are mostly quite general and resist any attempt to associate them with any particular gnostic group." (70)

The second -- and most important -- section of the "B source" is, according to Hedrick's outline, "The Third Appearance of the Illuminator." It consists of the material at CG V: 76,8-11; 76, 14-82,17; 82,19-83,4.(71) This section is especially relevant to the question of the possible "Christian intent" of the text.

> There are three motifs in this section that have been described as Christian: the illuminator suffers in his flesh, his converts are called "fruitbearing trees," and the illuminator performs signs and wonders....They appear here in a cluster, and this configuration raises the possibility that they are indirect references to Jesus, although the name of Jesus is not mentioned in the text. On this basis, arguments have been made that the section should be characterized as Christian.(72)

It is impossible to recapitulate here Hedrick's complex analysis of "how these [possibly Christian] motifs function in the myth in the <u>Apoc. Adam</u>."(73) The reader again may consult his full discussion for details.(74) I quote only his summary remarks on the matter. Their implications for the question at hand are quite clear.

> What is left after one disregards these...[possibly Christian] motifs, is a consistent narrative whose basic or primary structure not only remains intact, but perhaps is somewhat improved....The only observable change to the myth concerns its external character; that is, it no longer contains features suggestive of Christian influence. Therefore <u>I... characterize these three motifs with respect to function as secondary</u> features...not part of the primary structure of the narrative....<u>I would judge any characterization attributed to the total narrative under the influence of these... motifs to be...based upon secondary features...not constitutive of the narrative as a whole</u>. <u>The narrative should be characterized on the basis of its primary structure, and not on attendant or secondary motifs</u>....The presence of <u>these motifs gives the narrative a character different from the character of the narrative as a whole</u>....<u>The reader</u> [therefore] "sees" the text in a different light; that is...<u>views the text through the total spectrum of the Christian tradition, and is thereby misled as to its true or primary char-</u>

acter in that he attributes a character to the narrative...
not evident from its primary motives....A better approach to
the text is to interpret these motifs in harmony with the
nature of the text as a whole, <u>since the use of these motifs
is not restricted to the Christian tradition only</u>.(75)

It is clear that, in Hedrick's view, anyone who would impute any
true "Christian intent" to the writer(s) of this part of "the B
section" would be "misled"!

The discussion of possible "Christian intent" in <u>Apoc. Adam</u> --
as Hedrick views that text -- must, of course, take seriously
the "intent" of the final redactor. Hedrick's analysis of the
role of that redactor clearly disassociates him from "Christianity." He concludes that the final redaction of:

> The <u>Apoc. Adam</u> apparently was produced during an early stage
> of the Sethian-Archontic tradition by a minority group that
> argued for a spiritualized understanding of baptism and an
> ascetic lifestyle....The <u>evident lack of Christian influence</u>
> on the <u>Apoc. Adam</u> also corresponds...with the lack of Chris-
> tian influence on the Archontics as described by Epiphanius.
> Therefore it would seem that we must assume that the <u>Apoc.
> Adam</u> was redacted <u>in a time before the Sethian movement was
> Christianized</u>....(76)

There is no conceivable way one could conclude, from Hedrick's
study of <u>Apoc. Adam</u>, that any of the groups or individuals he
finds involved in its composition considered themselves "Christian" -- or their (its) doctrine "Christian." These past basic
analyses of <u>Apoc. Adam</u>, the most important of which are those of
MacRae and Hedrick, thus agree that it is a non-Christian text;
that is, it was not written by those who considered themselves
"Christian" and its "doctrine" as the really authentic version
of "Christian doctrine."(77) My own reading of the text suggests no reason to challenge that consensus. Therefore, even if
-- as is not <u>at all</u> certain -- the phrase "ⲟⲩⲅⲛⲱⲥⲓⲥⲛ̄[ⲧⲉ]ⲧⲙⲉ" at
83,13b-14a is a technical term, it could not be even <u>formally</u>
synonymous with the technical terms "ⲡⲥⲟⲟⲩⲛ̄ⲛ̄ⲧⲙⲏⲉ" and "ἐπίγνωσις
ἀληθείας": "everything involved in '<u>being Christian</u>.'"

At this time, before moving to the next stage of my argument in
the next chapter, it may be useful to recapitulate the points
already demonstrated. 1) The technical terms "ⲡⲥⲟⲟⲩⲛ̄ⲛ̄ⲧⲙⲏⲉ" in
<u>Thom. Cont.</u> and "ἐπίγνωσις ἀληθείας" in the Pastoral Epistles
are, when purely formally-defined, synonymous -- synonymous as
representations of "Christsein": "everything involved in 'being
Christian.'" 2) When, however, the actual "content definition"
of "ⲡⲥⲟⲟⲩⲛ̄ⲛ̄ⲧⲙⲏⲉ" demanded by the "basic teaching" of "section A"
of <u>Thom. Cont.</u> is compared with the actual "content definition"
of "ἐπίγνωσις ἀληθείας" demanded by the "basic teaching" of the
Pastorals, each -- every -- aspect of the technical meaning of
"ⲡⲥⲟⲟⲩⲛ̄ⲛ̄ⲧⲙⲏⲉ" is directly opposed by the corresponding aspect of

the technical meaning of "ἐπίγνωσις ἀληθείας." 3) The remarkable nature of the relationship between these technical terms appears even more striking when considered in light of the historical survey just concluded. That survey revealed no apparent precise parallel to the relationship between the two versions of "Christsein" represented by these two formally synonymous technical terms meaning "the knowledge of the truth."(78)

Chapter V
THE DOCTRINE OF THOMAS THE CONTENDER AND THE "FALSE TEACHINGS"

The "content definition" of "ⲡⲥⲟⲟⲩⲛ ⲛ̄ⲧⲙⲏⲉ" ("the knowledge of the truth") as "Christsein" which is so totally opposed by the Pastorals' understanding of "ἐπίγνωσις ἀληθείας" ("the knowledge of the truth") as "Christsein" was dictated by the "basic teaching" of "section A" of Thom. Cont. It can be demonstrated that the most important aspects of that "basic teaching" appear to correspond to the four most important elements of the "false teaching" attacked in the Pastorals. This correspondence is the reason I have suggested that evidence from Thom. Cont.: "...allows the Pastorals' struggle against false teaching to be viewed from an historical perspective not before available to New Testament scholarship." After this "correspondence" has been demonstrated I may then initially suggest the more specific two-part hypothesis which my analysis would also appear to allow.

I) Without any question the single most important element in the "basic teaching" of "section A" (and "section B") of Thom. Cont. is an extreme anti-sexual asceticism. Sexual activity and -- stated explicitly only in "section A" -- its result, offspring, are seen as paradigmatic of the basic "human problem" "the Savior" attempts to address. This point has surely already been adequately demonstrated and need not be outlined again here.

The Pastorals, of course, specifically attack those "who forbid marriage." (1 Tim. 4:3a) The positive injunctions which validate marriage, and/or the bearing of children, are even more significant in clearly implying that those being attacked opposed marriage and sexuality. "Yet women will be saved through bearing children...." "So I would have younger widows marry, bear children...."(1) It is obvious that the most important single element of the "basic teaching" in "section A" of Thom. Cont. is emphatically opposed as "false teaching" in the Pastorals.

II) Food-related asceticism, surely at least implicit in that "basic teaching" of "section A" which so emphasizes the intrinsically evil nature of all fleshly desires, is also attacked by the Pastorals. Such asceticism is directly attacked; and another positive injunction must be seen as an implicit rejection of that type of asceticism. The most directly relevant passage is, of course, that attacking those who "enjoin abstinence from foods." (1 Tim. 4:3) That statement is, moreover, immediately followed by a general affirmation of the goodness of God's created world. "For everything created by God is good, and nothing is to be rejected if it is received with thanksgiving...."(2) The fundamental point of view on the nature of the created world contained in "the Christian basic teaching" of "section A" of Thom. Cont. is directly opposed to the thrust of the Christian teaching at 1 Tim. 4:4.(3) Tit. 1:15 also could be taken as a rejection of <u>any</u> authentically Christian overall food-related asceticism. "To the pure all things are pure, but to the corrupt and unbelieving nothing is pure...."(4) Finally, the <u>positive</u> injunction at 1 Tim. 5:23 clearly implies basic opposition to excessive "dietary" asceticism. "No longer drink only water, but use a little wine for the sake of your stomach and your frequent ailments."

The false teaching attacked by the Pastorals thus clearly was characterized by asceticism with regard to both sexual activity and dietary consumption. Such false teachings obviously are essential parts of the "basic teaching" of "section A" of <u>Thom. Cont.</u>, the "basic teaching" which fixes the "content definition" of the technical term "ⲛⲥⲟⲟⲩⲛⲛ̄ⲧⲙⲏⲉ" as "Christsein."

III) A crucial element of the "basic teaching" in "section A" of <u>Thom. Cont.</u>, an element which affects <u>every</u> facet of the "content definition" of "ⲛⲥⲟⲟⲩⲛⲛ̄ⲧⲙⲏⲉ," is the view that "the Savior" himself does not even <u>desire</u> the salvation of <u>all</u> men. Universal salvation is not the divine will! The extremely emphatic way in which the Pastorals so firmly assert God's <u>desire</u> for universal salvation clearly suggests that a polemic against precisely such a view as that of "the Savior" in <u>Thom. Cont.</u> was also involved in the Pastorals' struggle against false teaching.

The statement at 1 Tim. 2:3-6a(5) is especially significant, for several reasons. 1) The divine desire to save <u>all</u> men could not possibly be stated more emphatically and unequivocally. The -- unequivocal in itself -- statement at 2:4 that God desires "all men" to be saved is followed, almost immediately, by the "ransom" statement already discussed at length. The significance of the use of "the expressly universal" "πάντων" in that statement, especially relevant to the matter now in question, was noted in that prior discussion. 2) The "unequivocal" statement at 2:4 is also intimately related to one of the -- polemically oriented -- technical usages of "ἐπίγνωσις ἀληθείας" analyzed by Dibelius in the article which initiated this entire investigation. 3) I have already quoted(6) secondary literature suggesting that the entire passage in question may be a specifically anti-Gnostic statement. 4) This passage, besides affirming God's desire for universal salvation, also stresses at least two other doctrines which are conspicuous by their absence in <u>Thom. Cont.</u>: the "incarnation" ("the man Christ Jesus"); the idea of Jesus Christ as a "ransom."

I must requote just two more passages in order to demonstrate the great emphasis the Pastorals place upon rejecting the teaching, so important in "section A" of <u>Thom. Cont.</u>, the view that "Christianity" demands the damnation of at least a portion of mankind. Tit. 2:11 contains an emphatic statement of God's <u>desire</u> to save all. "For the grace of God has appeared for the salvation of all men...." Finally, the passage Dibelius considered the most systematic and explicit "anti-heresy" statement in the Pastorals,(7) besides condemning the two types of asceticism already discussed, also contains a statement directly rejecting this third teaching which is so crucial to the ideology of "section A" of Thom. Cont. "The living God...is the Savior of all men...." (1 Tim. 4:10b) The third teaching emphatically attacked by the Pastorals as "false" ("heretical") is the view, crucial to "section A" of Thom. Cont., that universal salvation is not the divine desire!

IV) Even though it does not dominate "section A" of Thom. Cont. nearly so much as it does most "Gnostic" texts, the desire for "esoteric knowledge" -- "speculation" about such matters as "the Depth (βάθος) of the All" -- does play a role in its version of "Christianity." A survey of just the Pastoral texts Dibelius lists as devoted to the "Ketzerbekampfung"(8) reveals at least twelve statements deprecating such "speculation" -- or at least the "way of thinking" it reflects. Surely, therefore, a fourth important element in the false teaching attacked by the Pastorals involved idle "speculation" -- the "way of thinking" which would be concerned with such matters as "the Depth (βάθος) of the All."

The classic "anti-speculative" ("anti-Gnostic") passage must, of course, be cited here again: the denunciation of "the godless chatter and contradictions of what is falsely called knowledge." (1 Tim. 6:20-21) The other "anti-speculative" statements in the Pastorals may be divided basically into three groups. 1) One group refers to "speculation" in the context of the term "myths" ("μῦθοι"). 2) Another group seems to be basically pragmatically directed against (my wording): "dispute-causing, useless, esoteric -- usually otherwise undefined -- speculation." 3) The final group of statements is seemingly directed against types of "speculation" attributed to Jewish or "Judaizing" influence.(9)

The first category consists of the statements found at: 1 Tim. 1:4 (perhaps the most emphatic of this type); 1 Tim. 4:7; 2 Tim. 4:4. One must avoid: "myths and endless genealogies which promote speculations" (1 Tim. 1:4); "godless and silly myths" (1 Tim. 4:7);(10) the impulse to "turn away from...the truth and wander into myths." (2 Tim. 4:4) The second category consists of the statements at: 1 Tim. 6:4; 2 Tim. 2:14,16,23. At 1 Tim. 6:4 the "craving for controversy and for disputes about words" is deprecated. Similarly, a genuine Christian wastes his time in: "disputing about words" (2 Tim. 2:14); "godless chatter" (2 Tim. 2:16); "stupid, senseless controversies." (2 Tim. 2:23) What I call the Pastorals' "doctrine of doctrine" seems to represent, at least partially, a rejection of the types of thinking spoken of in the eight passages cited to this point -- their rejection in favor of "sober" "reasonableness," "sensibleness," etc.

All but one of the passages of the final type appear in Titus. At Tit. 1:10 "empty talkers and deceivers, especially [emphasis added] the circumcision party" are attacked. At Tit. 1:14 -- and only there -- the "myths" rejected are characterized as being "Jewish myths." At Tit. 3:9 the attack is upon "stupid controversies, genealogies, dissentions, and [emphasis added] quarrels over the law." It certainly would seem, however, that at Tit. 1:10 and 3:9 the polemic is not directed just at "Jewish" or "Judaizing" speculation. Finally, at 1 Tim. 1:6-7, the attack is upon: "Certain persons [who]...have wandered away into vain discussion, desiring to be teachers of the law...."

It is useful here to quote language from the English translation of "Dibelius" which describes the false teachers attacked in the Pastorals in these words:

> Characteristic are: speculations about the elements, but no systematic cosmology; a tendency toward soteriological dualism and the observation of ascetic rules. All this applies to the false teachers opposed by the Pastorals....(11)

These words describe the basic elements of the false teaching attacked in the Pastorals in a way which appears remarkably like a description of the most important elements found in the "basic teaching" of "section A" of Thom. Cont.!(12)

A fifth aspect of the false teaching attacked in the Pastorals, prominently mentioned in Dibelius's most systematic attempt to characterize the "Irrlehrer,"(13) is totally lacking in Thom. Cont. I refer to the doctrine that "the resurrection is past already." (2 Tim. 2:18) Thom. Cont., of course, contains no sort of doctrine of a "realized resurrection."

I would, however, argue strenuously that, according to the evidence from the Pastorals themselves, that particular doctrine constituted a much less significant aspect of the "false teaching" attacked than any of the four other teachings discussed to this point. A "realized resurrection" is only mentioned once -- at 2 Tim. 2:18. I would contend that the importance of the doctrine of a "realized resurrection" -- in the overall picture of the false teaching opposed by the Pastorals -- has been overemphasized because such a teaching was attributed to Menander by Justin(14) and Irenaeus(15); and because, more recently, such a "Valentinian" Gnostic teaching has been found (most clearly stated) in some Nag Hammadi texts.(16) I would still insist, therefore, that -- according to the Pastorals themselves -- the four most important aspects of the "false teaching" they attack correspond to parts of the "basic teaching" of "section A" of Thom. Cont.(17)

I have now attempted to demonstrate as clearly as possible the four fundamental points underlying the basic hypothesis I shall propose as the result of this study. In addition to the three points previously demonstrated, and recapitulated at the end of the previous chapter,(18) it should now be clear why I can also contend that: 4) The four crucial aspects of the "basic teaching" of "section A" of Thom. Cont., the teaching which fixes the "content definition" of "ⲡⲥⲟⲟⲩⲛ︦ⲧⲙⲏⲉ," appear to correspond very closely to the four most important elements of the "false teaching" attacked in the Pastorals' polemic -- the polemic in which "ἐπίγνωσις ἀληθείας" plays a quite significant role.

On the basis of these four fundamental points, I may now suggest this somewhat general two-part hypothesis as a thesis legitimately adduced from the evidence they provide. 1) It is quite possible that in "section A" of Thom. Cont. we find -- apparently for the first time -- an historical witness to an attested ideology representing the most important teachings attacked by the Pastorals as "false" ("heretical"). 2) The use of the term "ⲡⲥⲟⲟⲩⲛ︦ⲧⲙⲏⲉ" in Thom. Cont. also, therefore, very possibly represents an historical witness to a "heterodox" attempt to state the meaning of "the knowledge of the truth" -- as a technical term representing "everything involved in 'being Christian'" -- a technical term previously seen only from an "orthodox" point of view.

One more matter must be discussed in this chapter, rather fully, before I can outline some of the more detailed possible historical implications of the two-part hypothesis I have just suggested. The "basic teaching" of "section A" of Thom. Cont. -- which in other ways so well corresponds to the most important aspects of the false teaching attacked in the Pastorals -- does not appear to reflect any Jewish or "Judaizing" traits. What then is to be made of the fact that the Pastorals sometimes depict parts of that false teaching in contexts which seem to link them to Judaism or "Judaizing Christianity"?

I would contend, first of all, that many past analyses of the false teaching opposed by the Pastorals have vastly overemphasized its Jewish or "Judaizing" character. The extent to which the Pastorals' polemic characterizes the false teachings as reflecting Jewish or "Judaizing" tendencies is really not at all that great! It seems clear that, to say the least, the false teachings are not represented as being essentially or basically of a Jewish or "Judaizing" nature! I have described five basic aspects of that false teaching. Three of these five aspects of the false teaching are never attacked in a context in any way relating them either to Judaism or "Judaizing Christianity."

1) The teaching about a "realized resurrection" (2 Tim. 2:18) which, in any case is not found in Thom. Cont., bears no relationship to any known "Judaizing" or Jewish ideology. 2) A most important aspect of the false teaching opposed in the Pastorals' polemic, the single most important part of the ideology of "section A" of Thom. Cont., is sexual asceticism. The passages involved in the Pastorals, the attack upon those "who forbid marriage" (1 Tim. 4:3a), supported by the positive injunctions regarding marriage and/or the bearing of children (1 Tim. 2:15a;

5:14a), never relate this false teaching to Judaism or to any sort of "Judaizing" tendency. This fact is, since Judaism holds a basically positive view of rightly-displayed sexuality, not at all surprising. 3) The Pastorals' frequent, unequivocal assertions of God's desire for universal salvation indicate clearly that an important element of the false teaching opposed was some doctrine that not all should be saved -- the teaching of "the Savior" in "section A" of Thom. Cont. which affects every aspect of the "content definition" of "ⲡⲥⲟⲟⲩⲛ̄ⲛ̄ⲧⲙⲏⲉ"! The contexts in which these emphatic statements about the desirability of universal salvation (1 Tim. 2:3-4,6; 4:10; Tit. 2:11) appear give no reason, however, to suggest that Judaism or "Judaizing" was involved in the matter in question. Three of the five aspects of the false teaching opposed by the Pastorals -- including the two most strikingly characteristic of "section A" of Thom. Cont. -- are, therefore, never spoken of in a way which appears to reflect controversy with Jewish or "Judaizing" "false teachers"!

The Pastorals' polemic against two aspects of the false teaching can, however, be taken -- in some cases -- as attacks upon ideas depicted as Jewish or "Judaizing" phenomena. One of the four passages attacking food-related asceticism appears in a context indicating that it probably reflects an attack upon the Jewish dietary law. Four of the twelve passages attacking idle "speculation" or the desire for "esoteric knowledge" appear in apparently anti-Jewish or "anti-Judaizing" contexts.

It is probable that the language at Tit. 1:13-15 contains an attack upon food rejection associated with the Jewish dietary law. (19) I have already quoted Tit. 1:15 as an attack upon food-related asceticism: "To the pure all things are pure, but to the corrupt and unbelieving nothing is pure...." This statement immediately follows advice to "rebuke" those who give: "...heed to Jewish myths or to commands of men...." (Tit. 1:13b-14) In context, especially in light of the deprecation of the "circumcision party" at Tit. 1:10,(20) "commands of men" would seem a reference to the (Jewish) dietary law; the language at Tit. 1:15 would, therefore, appear to be an attack upon food-related asceticism depicted as a "Judaizing" phenomenon.

Nevertheless, the other three passages involved in the Pastoral polemic against food-related (dietary) asceticism give -- in my opinion -- no clear indication at all that the asceticism opposed is depicted as a Jewish or "Judaizing" phenomenon. There is no reason to take the direct attack upon those who "enjoin abstinence from foods" (1 Tim. 4:3) as an anti-Jewish or "anti-Judaizing" statement. That attack, moreover, clearly refers to the same persons rebuked in that verse for forbidding marriage. It has already been pointed out that there is no reason to take the polemic against those "who forbid marriage" as anti-Jewish. The more general statement in the next verse,(21) which in context is apparently meant to refer especially to food, seems unrelated to any anti-Jewish or "anti-Judaizing" polemic. Exactly the same may be said of the positive injunction at 1 Tim. 5:23 implicitly rejecting this sort of asceticism: "Use a little wine ...."

The polemic against "esoteric thinking" or "speculation" found at 1 Tim. 1:6b-7; Tit. 1:10,14; 3:9 seems to represent that phenomenon as related to Judaism or "Judaizing Christianity." At 1 Tim. 1:6b-7 the attack is directed at those who: "...have wandered away into vain discussion, desiring to be teachers of the law [emphasis added]...." At Tit. 1:10 the rebuke is similarly directed against: "...empty talkers and deceivers, especially the circumcision party...."(22) The specific reference to "Jewish [emphasis added] myths" at Tit. 1:14 has also already been noted. Finally, one is urged at Tit. 3:9 to "avoid stupid controversies, genealogies, dissentions, and [emphasis added] quarrels over the law...." One-third of the passages in the Pastorals attacking "speculation" or "esoteric thinking" seem, therefore, to depict this error as related to Judaism or "Judaizing Christianity." Even if this were the case, eight of the twelve passages attacking this aspect of the false teaching give no indication that the phenomenon was seen as related to Judaism or "Judaizing" thought. At the least, therefore, it can be safely said that the Pastorals do not depict this "speculative" aspect of the false teaching as purely -- or even primarily -- a Jewish or "Judaizing" phenomenon.

The anti-Jewish orientation of the polemic in three of the four passages noted, however, is not, in fact, nearly so unequivocal as it might first appear. The words "and" ("καί") and "especially" ("μάλιστα") have been emphasized in my quotation of Tit. 3:9 and Tit. 1:10 in order to indicate my view that those two passages really are meant to deprecate "speculation in general" -- some elements of which are then specified as being related to Judaism or "Judaizing Christianity." Even one of the passages which apparently unequivocally identifies the evil "speculation" with Judaism is not, according to Dibelius's interpretation, at all "unequivocal" in that regard. That is, at Tit. 1:14:

> Die Betonung der ἐντολαί ἀνθρώπων (vgl. Col 2 8. 22?) könnte den Verdacht rechtfertigen, dass bei Ἰουδαϊκοί mehr an die Art als an die Herkunft gedacht werden müsse....μῦθος wäre dann farblos zu nehmen s. I Tim 1 4....(23)

This interpretation of "Jewish myths" at Tit. 1:14 -- as related to the meaning of "μῦθοις" at 1 Tim. 1:4 -- is significant for two reasons. It would, of course, radically diminish the "anti-Judaizing" character of the polemic at Tit. 1:14-15, the passage apparently most suggestive of a relationship between the false teaching opposed and "Judaizing Christianity." Moreover, if the polemic use of "μῦθος" -- in the one passage in which that term is specifically associated with Judaism -- does not represent "μῦθος" as designating a particularly "Judaizing" type of error, an "anti-Judaizing" interpretation can certainly not be given to all the other polemic usages of "μῦθος" describing the error of "speculation." That is, in the other passages in question, "myths" can not at all necessarily really mean: "Jewish myths."

Three of the five aspects of the false teaching attacked by the Pastorals -- including the two most clearly characteristic of the thought of "section A" of Thom. Cont. -- are never designated as being related to Judaism or "Judaizing Christianity." It is probable that one of the four Pastoral attacks upon dietary asceticism associates it with the Jewish dietary law. At the most, one-third of the passages deprecating "speculation" relate that phenomenon -- to some degree at least -- to Judaism or "Judaizing" tendencies. Just these factors indicate the relatively insignificant degree to which the false teaching opposed by the Pastorals is characterized as Jewish or "Judaizing."

The analysis of the extent to which the Pastorals characterize the false teachings as "Jewish" or "Judaizing" must, moreover, take another factor into consideration. Dibelius pointed out, with specific regard to the Pastorals' attack on food-related asceticism: "schliesslich konnte jede Nahrungsaskese...von den Christen 'Judaismus' genannt werden."(24) The extent to which a young religion still differentiating itself from its Jewish parent would tend -- consciously or unconsciously -- to exaggerate the "Jewishness" of any teaching even faintly resembling the Judaism with which Christianity was still in conflict must be kept in mind! If, as Dibelius suggested, any "food asceticism" might be called "Judaism," why could the "Jewish" character of the "speculative" aspect of the false teaching opposed not also have been represented in an exaggerated fashion? In light of the Sitz-im-Leben, might not the writer(s) of the Pastorals tend to overcharacterize the "Jewish" nature of any "false teaching" being opposed?(25)

The two aspects of the false teaching attacked by the Pastorals which are most important to the doctrine of Thom. Cont. (sexual asceticism, a doctrine that universal salvation is not even the divine desire) are never characterized as Jewish or "Judaizing." The two other most important aspects of the false teaching the Pastorals opposed ("speculation," food-related asceticism) are treated in an anti-Jewish, or "anti-Judaizing," context far less often -- to say the least -- than they are not. In the context of the Pastorals' Sitz-im-Leben, the extent to which those two teachings are characterized as "Jewish" may quite possibly exaggerate their real relationship to Judaism or "Judaizing Christianity." I, therefore -- in light of the striking similarities already suggested -- can not see why the really fundamental aspects of the false teaching attacked by the Pastorals could not be represented, more than one hundred years later, in "section A" of Thom. Cont. with their originally quite weak Jewish orientation having been totally lost. Such a relatively inconsequential element in the false teachings opposed by the Pastorals, which otherwise fit the basic ideas of "section A" of Thom.

Cont. so well, could simply have gradually been lost sight of during the century between the writing of the Pastorals and the writing of the <u>Vorlage</u> of "section A." The apparent problem of the totally non-Jewish character of "section A" of <u>Thom. Cont.</u> is quite explicable on the basis of this argument alone.

I must, nevertheless, at least suggest an additional <u>possible</u> explanation which I would consider a legitimate implication of George W. MacRae's basic view of Gnostic origins. He has recently stated:

> ...I believe that Gnosticism arose as a revolutionary reaction in Hellenized Jewish wisdom and apocalyptic circles. It became a rival of Christianity not...in the second century when the ecclesiastical writers such as...Irenaeus identified Gnostic leaders and sects, but <u>from the very beginnings of Christian reflection on the significance and message of Jesus.</u>(26)

He, therefore, considers Gnosticism historically as: "<u>not</u> [originally] <u>a Christian heresy but if anything a Jewish heresy</u> [or set of heresies], <u>just as primitive Christianity itself should be regarded as a Jewish heresy or set of Jewish heresies.</u>"(27) According to MacRae's hypothesis, these statements could, therefore, be made. 1) Christianity arose from Judaism as a "heresy" -- because of the meaning "Christians" derived from "reflection on the significance and message of Jesus." 2) "Gnosticism" also arose from Judaism, approximately contemporaneously with "Christianity," as another "heresy." 3) "Gnosticism," however, represented a radically (esoteric) speculatively oriented development of trends in current Jewish "wisdom and apocalyptic circles."

MacRae believes that one does not find an "authentic Christian Gnosticism" until "Valentinianism."(28) Nevertheless, he cites many examples of interaction between the two "Jewish heresies" from their very beginnings. He clearly suggests that <u>Paul</u> -- the earliest New Testament writer -- may well have been influenced by "Gnostic" motifs.(29) MacRae, moreover, specifically notes "the natural affinity [of Gnosticism and Christianity] arising from a certain common [Jewish] parentage."(30) I, therefore, see nothing in his argument demanding one to deny that, by the time the Pastorals were written, the two "heresies" in question were not already sometimes to be found in a "mixed" form -- such as that represented by the most important elements of the false teaching attacked in those epistles.

One might, therefore, at least hypothesize -- on the basis of MacRae's view of the origins of the "Christian Jewish heresy" and the "Gnostic Jewish heresy" -- this explanation to the question raised in this latter part of the chapter. The Pastorals' polemic, to the extent to which it describes the false teachings as "Jewish-Gnostic" threats to Christianity, might actually represent the conflict between a "single Jewish heresy" -- "Christianity" -- and a "double Jewish heresy," that is, "primitive Gnostic Christianity." Then the "single heretics" from Judaism (in the Pastorals) would oppose such a "double heresy" for two reasons. It included an extra, erroneous element -- speculative "primitive Gnosticism." Simultaneously, however, it was seen as <u>not being heretical enough</u> in the degree to which it <u>rejected the Judaism</u> from which Christianity had risen in revolt. A century later, however, the group responsible for "section A" of <u>Thom. Cont.</u>, as descendants of "Gnostic heretics" <u>against</u> Judaism, could have inherited -- in a totally non-Jewish context -- the same fundamental ideas opposed by the Pastorals. That is, the intervening century might have seen a <u>conscious</u> obliteration of all ideological linkage to the rejected parent of the "heresy."

Such an extension of the (possible) implications of MacRae's basic hypothesis regarding Gnostic origins could, therefore, also account for the fact that the most important false teachings attacked by the Pastorals -- occasionally in an anti-Jewish context -- appear, in a totally non-Jewish context, as the most essential elements of the "basic teaching" found in "section A" of <u>Thom. Cont.</u> I must reiterate, however, that this latter argument, which some readers may find an undue extension of the logical implications of MacRae's views (although I personally find it quite possibly viable), is not at all essential to the final conclusions of this study. I have given another argument, quite independent of this personal hypothesis, which makes the "apparent problem" in question "quite explicable."(31) Therefore, the fact that the Pastorals occasionally characterize some aspects of the false teachings they struggle against as "Jewish," or as "Judaizing," presents no real problem for the final hypothesis I see as the logical conclusion suggested by this study.

Chapter VI
SUMMARY AND CONCLUSIONS:
THE POSSIBLE HISTORICAL IMPLICATIONS

For the sake of absolute clarity I again recapitulate the (now) five points already demonstrated which provide the basis for the two-part hypothesis I have proposed as the logical conclusion of this study -- some of the more detailed implications of which I can, at this time, also describe. I) The two technical terms, "ⲡⲥⲟⲟⲩⲛ ⲛ̄ⲧⲙⲏⲉ" ("the knowledge of the truth") in "section A" of Thomas the Contender, and "ἐπίγνωσις ἀληθείας" ("the knowledge of the truth") in the Pastoral Epistles -- when defined purely formally -- are totally synonymous expressions for "Christsein": "everything involved in 'being Christian.'" II) When these two formally synonymous expressions are given the "content definitions" of "everything involved in 'being Christian'" demanded by the "basic teachings" of "section A" of Thom. Cont. and the Pastorals, every facet of the meaning of "ⲡⲥⲟⲟⲩⲛ ⲛ̄ⲧⲙⲏⲉ" is opposed -- diametrically -- by the corresponding aspect of the meaning of "ἐπίγνωσις ἀληθείας." III) A historical survey of the religious and philosophical usage, in the Greco-Roman world and in the Nag Hammadi corpus of possibly technical terms meaning "the knowledge of the truth," yielded no precise parallel to the relationship between the versions of "Christsein" represented by the two formally synonymous terms "ⲡⲥⲟⲟⲩⲛ ⲛ̄ⲧⲙⲏⲉ" and "ἐπίγνωσις ἀληθείας."(1) IV) The "basic teaching" of "section A" of Thom. Cont. which determines the "content definition" of "ⲡⲥⲟⲟⲩⲛ ⲛ̄ⲧⲙⲏⲉ" as "Christsein" -- the "content definition" directly opposed by the "content definition" of "ἐπίγνωσις ἀληθείας" as "Christsein" in the Pastorals -- very closely corresponds to the four most important parts of the teaching attacked by the Pastorals as being "false." V) Although parts of that false teaching are sometimes characterized by the Pastorals as representing Jewish (or "Judaizing") phenomena, the totally non-Jewish context in which the corresponding elements of the "basic teaching" in "section A" of Thom. Cont. appear is easily explicable on historical bases of fundamentally inconsequential "ideological" significance.

All of these factors suggest the two-part hypothesis to which I have already briefly alluded. 1) We may well see, in the ideology of the group responsible for "section A" of Thom. Cont. -- apparently for the first time -- a historical witness to an actually attested ideology bearing remarkable resemblance to the most important aspects of the teachings attacked as "false" by the Pastorals. 2) The use of "ⲡⲥⲟⲟⲩⲛ ⲛ̄ⲧⲙⲏⲉ" in Thom. Cont. may well also be a historical witness to the heterodox use of "the knowledge of the truth" as a technical term for "Christsein" -- technical usage previously detected only in "orthodox" efforts to define "Christsein." I can offer only limited further explication of the first part of my hypothesis. The second part, however, allows me to discuss some rather intriguing historical possibilities.

The initial part of my hypothesis does not, first of all, assume -- as appears quite unlikely in any case -- that one "sect," or unified group of any sort, was responsible for all of the various aspects of the false teachings opposed by the Pastorals. I also do not mean to imply that the ideology of the group responsible for "section A" of <u>Thom. Cont.</u> was totally identical to even the (probably) "composite" false teaching represented in the Pastorals.(2) I, however, still find it remarkable -- and a fact quite worthy of being called to attention -- that one can see in "section A" of <u>Thom. Cont.</u> a configuration of ideas ("basic teaching"), which <u>is historically attested</u>, and which is so very like the most important aspects of the teachings attacked by the Pastorals! That configuration of ideas -- "basic teaching" -- is so like those false teachings that one might even describe the version of "Christsein" represented by "ⲡⲥⲟⲟⲩⲛ︤ⲛ︦ⲧⲙⲏⲉ" as <u>looking very much like</u> an "ideological descendent" of those teachings attacked by the Pastorals. While such a "causal" relationship between the teaching described in the Pastorals and the "basic teaching" of "section A" of <u>Thom. Cont.</u> is obviously unprovable, I still reiterate that it is quite significant for New Testament scholarship that in "section A" of <u>Thom. Cont.</u> one does find a witness to an actually historically attested ideology which represents the most important teachings attacked as "false" by the Pastorals. The possible further implications of that statement should be the subject of future study by specialists in the Pastorals. As a Nag Hammadi specialist I have simply pointed out this new evidence from <u>Thom. Cont.</u> which should be taken into account in future studies of the "false teachers" opposed in the Pastorals.

I can say much more about the possible implications of the second part of my hypothesis. It seems quite reasonable to suggest that the technical use of "ⲡⲥⲟⲟⲩⲛ︤ⲛ︦ⲧⲙⲏⲉ" in <u>Thom. Cont.</u> represents a continuation, a later stage of a discussion about the meaning of "the knowledge of the truth" seen from the orthodox side in the Pastorals' polemic use of "ἐπίγνωσις ἀληθείας." The usage of that term in the Pastorals clearly represents an orthodox attempt to employ "the knowledge of the truth" as a polemic technical term which was meant to represent "everything involved in <u>authentically</u> 'being Christian.'" "ⲡⲥⲟⲟⲩⲛ︤ⲛ︦ⲧⲙⲏⲉ" in "section A" of <u>Thom. Cont.</u> also seems to represent "the knowledge of the truth" as a technical term meaning "everything involved in <u>authentically</u> 'being Christian.'" In light of the affinity between the ideology which defines the meaning of "ⲡⲥⲟⲟⲩⲛ︤ⲛ︦ⲧⲙⲏⲉ" in <u>Thom. Cont.</u> and the (probably) then-composite configuration of the teaching(s) attacked by the Pastoral usage of "the knowledge of the truth," it seems <u>quite</u> possible -- (to say the least) -- that the use of "ⲡⲥⲟⲟⲩⲛ︤ⲛ︦ⲧⲙⲏⲉ" in "section A" of <u>Thom. Cont.</u> represents <u>a conscious heterodox attempt to define correctly</u> "the knowledge of the truth" -- as a (technical) term representing: "everything involved in <u>authentically</u> 'being Christian.'"

More specifically, the Pastorals had insisted, by their definition of "the knowledge of the truth," that "authentically 'being Christian'" involved: affirmation of the goodness of creation and the rightness of its reasonable enjoyment; belief in God's desire for universal salvation; avoiding arrogant "speculation" about the deeper mysteries of God's universe. The self-identification, by "the Savior," with "ⲡⲥⲟⲟⲩⲛⲛ̄ⲧⲙⲏⲉ" in "section A" of Thom. Cont. would then indicate, however, that those responsible for "section A" insisted -- by their definition of "the knowledge of the truth" -- that "authentically 'being Christian'" actually consisted precisely of: the knowledge that the world and any "enjoyment" of it were evil; acceptance of the divine will that some men were justly doomed; seeking knowledge of the very deepest mysteries of the universe.

Since it is quite impossible to determine whether the Vorlage of "ⲡⲥⲟⲟⲩⲛⲛ̄ⲧⲙⲏⲉ" contained the Greek "γνῶσις" or "ἐπίγνωσις," the precise "methodology" used in Thom. Cont. to define correctly "the knowledge of the truth" could, therefore, have taken either of two forms. 1) If controversy with "Gnostics" had indeed already "discredited" the word "γνῶσις," as Dibelius suggested, those represented by the thought of "section A" of Thom. Cont. -- so ideologically related to the type of thinking attacked by "ἐπίγνωσις ἀληθείας" in the Pastorals -- could certainly have used the phrase "γνῶσις ἀληθείας" in order both to: reclaim the term "γνῶσις" as the "creditable" word to speak of "the knowledge of the truth"; and to define "γνῶσις ἀληθείας" according to their view of "authentically 'being Christian.'" Also, approximately contemporaneously with the writing of the Greek Vorlage of our text of Thom. Cont., Hippolytus did use "ἀληθείας γνώσει" as a technical term having the same formally-defined facets of meaning as "ⲡⲥⲟⲟⲩⲛⲛ̄ⲧⲙⲏⲉ" and "ἐπίγνωσις ἀληθείας" -- and used it to attack teachings having some fairly considerable affinities with at least the "way of thinking" represented in "section A" of Thom. Cont. It is at least possible, therefore, if the Vorlage of "ⲡⲥⲟⲟⲩⲛⲛ̄ⲧⲙⲏⲉ" was "(ἡ) γνῶσις (τῆς) ἀληθείας," that a continued orthodox polemic use of "the knowledge of the truth" -- employing the more common term "γνῶσις" in this case -- might also have been part of the total background for this "heterodox" usage of "the knowledge of the truth" in Thom. Cont. 2) If, on the other hand, the Vorlage of "ⲡⲥⲟⲟⲩⲛⲛ̄ⲧⲙⲏⲉ" consisted of "ἐπίγνωσις ἀληθείας," that usage might well reflect an attempt to validate the basic position attacked by the Pastoral use of that phrase -- to assert its "correct" meaning as a term representing "everything involved in authentically 'being Christian'"!

The basic two-part hypothesis I have proposed -- the details of which, it has been seen, may have several possible manifestations -- seems to represent the most plausible explanation for the peculiar relationship between the technical terms "ἐπίγνωσις ἀληθείας" in the Pastorals and "ⲡⲥⲟⲟⲩⲛⲛ̄ⲧⲙⲏⲉ" in Thom. Cont. I certainly do not claim to have "solved" the problem of the exact nature of the polemic struggle reflected in the Pastorals. As I have already pointed out, the full implications of the first part of my hypothesis will especially require the future work of specialists in the Pastorals. I simply suggest, as stated at the outset, that in the Nag Hammadi <u>corpus</u> (in <u>Thom. Cont.</u>) one quite possibly finds new evidence which will allow the Pastorals' struggle against "false teachers" to be legitimately viewed "from an historical perspective not before available to New Testament scholarship."

NOTES

INTRODUCTION

1) This study represents the final results of research begun for a short paper read 23 Sept., 1980 at the Second International Congress of Coptic Studies, Rome. The Book of Thomas the Contender (hereafter cited in text and notes as Thom. Cont.) is found at CG II: 138,1-145,19. The Coptic of the tractate is now available in The Facsimile Edition of the Nag Hammadi Codices: Codex II, 150-57. The first establishment of the text, accompanied by an English translation and extensive commentary, was that of John D. Turner: "The Book of Thomas the Contender from Codex II of the Cairo Gnostic Library from Nag Hammadi (CG II,7): The Coptic Text with Translation, Introduction and Commentary" (Ph.D. diss., Duke University, 1970). Turner's dissertation will be cited in its slightly revised published form, The Book of Thomas the Contender from Codex II of the Cairo Gnostic Library from Nag Hammadi (CG II,7). Turner's monograph is, by far, the most detailed study of Thom. Cont. to date. The principal reviews of his work have been those by: B. Layton, in Revue Biblique 83 (1976), 462-63; Hans Quecke, Biblica 57 (1976), 429-32; D.W. Johnson, Catholic Biblical Quarterly 39 (1977), 163-65; Malcolm L. Peel, Journal of the American Academy of Religion 45 (1977), 510-11; Pheme Perkins, Journal of Biblical Literature 96 (1977), 150-51; H. Chadwick, Journal of Theological Studies 29 (1978), 554-55. Martin Krause and Pahor Labib have also established the text, and provided a German translation, in Gnostische und hermetische Schriften aus Codex II und Codex VI, 88-106 (hereafter cited as Gnost. herm. Schriften). Krause has published a German translation of Thom. Cont., along with a brief introduction to the text, now available in English in Werner Foerster, comp., Gnosis; a Selection of Gnostic Texts, vol. 2, Coptic, and Mandic Sources, 110-18 (hereafter cited as Coptic Sources). Krause's introduction there stresses the basically "gnostic" character of the text, calling its doctrine: "...with the exception of a very few concepts known from the New Testament...purely gnostic...." (Ibid., 110). Turner has more recently published a slightly revised form of his earlier English translation, and a brief but useful introduction to Thom. Cont., in The Nag Hammadi Library in English, 188-94 (hereafter cited throughout as NH. in English, accompanied by the name of the particular contributor in question). D. Kircher has also published a German translation of the text, with a brief introduction which questions Turner's redaction analysis of the tractate ("'Das Buch des Thomas'," 793-804). Finally, Turner has summarized, and in some ways further developed, parts of his dissertation's basic argument in his "A New Link in the Syrian Judas Thomas Tradition," 109-19.

2) <u>Book of Thomas</u>, 5, 106-07, 110-12, 220-25, 238 <u>et Passim</u>; "New Link," 111, 115-17 <u>et Passim</u>.
3) Turner's detailed redaction analysis in <u>Book of Thomas</u> (summarized in "New Link") has, at the least, certainly adduced enough evidence for the <u>basic</u> division of the text into two parts, a dialogue ("section A") and a monologue ("section B"), that it appears presumptuous to dismiss that <u>basic</u> division of the text -- as Malcolm Peel has done (review of <u>Book of Thomas</u>, <u>Journal of the American Academy of Religion</u> 45 [1977], 511) -- as a hypothesis which can be safely ignored in considering the document. See, for Turner's basic redaction argument, <u>Book of Thomas</u>, 5, 106-10 <u>et Passim</u>; and "New Link." I do not disagree, however, with the reviewers of <u>Book of Thomas</u> who have suggested that many <u>details</u> of Turner's analysis are highly questionable (e.g., some of his conjectures regarding interpolations introduced by the final redactor into each of the "sources"). At least two significant aspects of Turner's redaction analysis have, in my own opinion, been the object of cogent criticism: his assertions about the nature of the Coptic dialect in the "<u>incipit</u>" (See Hans Quecke, review of <u>Book of Thomas</u>, <u>Biblica</u> 57 [1976], 431.); his translation of the final lines of the text. (See Kircher, "Buch des Thomas," 802.) Although Turner employs both of these challenged arguments in support of his basic redaction analysis, I can not see that the <u>basic</u> division of the text into a dialogue and a monologue <u>is dependent on</u> either of those arguments. The literary forms (dialogue, monologue) of the two sections are totally different. The two sections differ radically in their use of certain technical terms; important motifs are unique to each section, etc. (See, for examples of such phenomena, Turner, <u>Book of Thomas</u>, 109-10.)
4) Turner, <u>Book of Thomas</u>, 5. My statement that <u>Thom. Cont.</u> "was composed by those who considered themselves and their doctrine 'Christian'" is an absolutely fundamental presupposition of this study which will be alluded to frequently throughout. The writers of the text relied upon, for their ultimate and saving revelation of "the truth," a "Savior" who -- as was just pointed out -- is <u>clearly</u> meant to represent Jesus Christ. In his two-page introduction to <u>Thom. Cont.</u> in <u>Coptic Sources</u> Krause uses the name "Jesus" eight times to refer to the text's revealer figure. It is thus obvious that the term "Christian" (at the very least as that adjective would be defined formally) may certainly legitimately be applied to them and the doctrine revealed to them by that "Savior." Krause's remarks concerning the basically "gnostic" character of the text (See note 1.) simply reflect what I have just called the "aberrant" nature of the type of "Christianity" reflected in <u>Thom. Cont.</u>
5) Martin Dibelius, "ἐπίγνωσις ἀληθείας."
6) He specifically suggested: "Dass der Gebrauch der fraglichen Worte in den Pastoralbriefen technisch ist, ergibt sich aus den Ketzerabschnitten der Briefe" (<u>Ibid.</u>, 1).

CHAPTER I

1) Martin Dibelius, "ἐπίγνωσις ἀληθείας," 2. Rudolph Bultmann has also noted: "It is just as hard to find any strict distinction between γνῶσις and ἐπίγνωσις in the NT as it is in the LXX and Philo" (Gerhard Kittel, ed., <u>Theological Dictionary of the New Testament</u>, 1: 707 [cited as <u>TDNT</u> hereafter, accompanied by the name of the particular contributor in question]).
2) Dibelius, "ἐπίγνωσις ἀληθείας," 2-3.
3) "Man könnte der Scheu vor dem bereits diskreditierten Worte γνῶσις (s. 1. Tim 6, 20) die Schuld geben" (<u>Ibid.</u>, 3).
4) <u>Ibid.</u>
5) <u>Ibid.</u>, 2.
6) "Die Briefe das Christsein mit der Formel ἐπίγνωσις ἀληθείας umschreiben" (<u>Ibid.</u>).
7) <u>Ibid.</u>
8) <u>Ibid.</u>
9) <u>Ibid.</u>
10) On the "καί explicative" see Walter Bauer, <u>A Greek-English Lexicon of the New Testament and Other Early Christian Literature</u>, 393 (hereafter cited as <u>BGD</u>).
11) Martin Dibelius, <u>Die Pastoralbriefe</u>, 2d rev. ed., 25; emphasis added. (All underlining in quotations, except where -- as here -- otherwise indicated, represents italics in the material quoted.) In considering Dibelius's complete exegesis of the Pastorals I have relied primarily upon this second edition of his commentary, the last edition actually revised by Dibelius himself. Some sections of the later German editions "revised" by Conzelmann, as well as parts of the augmented English translation of the last German edition, are so thoroughly "revised" that it is difficult to call "Dibelius" the "author." These later editions will be cited, of course, when they do contain additional material relevant to the purposes of this study.
12) The exegesis of the other passages supporting this conclusion may be found in my dissertation (Jesse Jeremiah Sell, "A Study of the Self-Predication Statements Attributed to 'Jesus Christ' in the Naga-Hammadi Coptic 'Gnostic' <u>Corpus</u>" [Ph.D. diss., Duke University, 1976], 79-82).
13) 2 Tim. 2:25-26a. All quotations from the English Bible, unless otherwise indicated, are taken from the Revised Standard Version. All quotations from the Greek New Testament, unless otherwise indicated, are taken from Erwin Nestle and Kurt Aland, eds., <u>Novum Testamentum Graece</u>, 25th ed. (Stuttgart: Würtembergische Bibelanstalt, 1963).
14) 2 Tim. 2:25b; my translation.
15) See note 10 above on the "καί explicative" ("that is"); my translation, emphasis added.
16) It will be recalled that Dibelius cited 2 Tim. 2:25 as one of the passages in which "ἐπίγνωσις ἀληθείας" represented

"des vollen Heilsstandes" (Pastoralbriefe, 2d rev. ed., 25).
17) The same formal definition would seem to fit the articular phrase at Heb. 10:26. Since that passage is basically peripheral to the purpose of this study, it will, however, not be further discussed.
18) CG II: 138,12b-13a. In the argument to follow, unless indicated otherwise, all quotation of Thom. Cont. represents my translation, based upon my transcription of the text from the facsimile edition of Codex II.
19) A similar complex and lengthy argument could be made from the logical relationship between the various parts of 138, 7-21 to demonstrate the facet of the term's meaning which refers to its being "intimately related to 'being saved.'" To include that argument here would, however, make this section of the study inordinately lengthy. On the other hand, I have two reasons for offering here the more complex argument related to the term's reference to "correct Christian doctrine." 1) It is almost necessary to provide the background for demonstrating the third facet of the formal meaning of "ⲡⲥⲟⲟⲩⲛⲛ̄ⲧⲙⲏⲉ," which has not yet been otherwise demonstrated. 2) This more complex argument regarding the term and its reference to "correct Christian doctrine" should, without unduly lengthening this section, also enable one to see that an analogously argued case could be made for the "soteriological" aspect of the term's meaning -- thus reinforcing the argument for it based upon the (formal) interchangeability of the terms already noted.
20) All underlining in this section represents, of course, my emphasis added.
21) See below on "βάθος" as a technical term. "The All" (often appearing in Nag Hammadi texts in the form "ⲡⲧⲏⲣϥ") is, of course, one of the most common Gnostic technical terms used to refer to ultimate, "esoteric" knowledge (of the pleroma, etc.).
22) Pheme Perkins (review of Book of Thomas, Journal of Biblical Literature 96 [1977], 150-51) has questioned Turner's translation of 138,16-21 for reasons which would also be applicable to my translation. Krause's translations (Gnost. herm. Schriften, 89; Coptic Sources, 112) appear to interpret that passage in accord with Perkins and against Turner and myself. I see no compelling reason their view need be preferred to that reflected in my, and Turner's translations. The two views appear at least equally viable. Nevertheless, I should note her critique here and, more importantly, point out that -- if she should be correct -- her view of 138,16-21 would in no way invalidate my argument regarding the way in which the logic of the development of that speech indicates that, formally-defined, "ⲡⲥⲟⲟⲩⲛⲛ̄ⲧⲙⲏⲉ" represents an "understanding" of "correct Christian doctrine" which also "necessarily expresses itself in one's way of life." She suggests that 138,16b-17a should be taken as the conclusion of the preceding sentence, rather than as the beginning of a new sentence. According to her interpretation, my transla-

tion of "parts 8-10" should be: "...you have already known and you will be called 'the one who knows himself'; because (γάρ) the one who has not known himself has not known anything. But [or "And"] (δέ) the one who has known himself also has already grasped knowledge of the Depth (βάθος) of the All." This difference in the way the text is divided into English sentences in no way changes the meaning of the passage. Adopting her view, I could still legitimately assert the point: "If one who has not known himself has known nothing, the contrary state [following the adversative, or conjunctive, "δέ"] of the one who does know himself (because he has known 'ⲡⲥⲟⲟⲩⲛⲛ̄ⲧⲙⲏⲉ') would seem clearly that of one who knows 'everything (of import)' ["correct Christian doctrine"]." Her interpretation, of course, would do nothing to diminish the impression, supporting my conclusion, lent the passage by the "impressive language": "knowledge of the Depth (βάθος) of the All." Her second objection to Turner's (and my) interpretation of those lines is that, at 138,19 "ⲛ̄ⲧⲟⲕ ⲡⲁⲥⲟⲛ̄ ⲑⲱⲙⲁⲥ," should not be translated as a nominal sentence ("You are my brother, Thomas.") but -- as "you, my brother, Thomas" -- should be instead taken as the subject of the final sentence of the speech. That is, my translation should be, in her opinion: "On account of this you, my brother, Thomas have seen that which is hidden from [other] men, that is, that which they stumble on -- they not knowing [it]." If, again, her view is accepted, it makes no difference whatsoever regarding my point that: "He [Thomas] has 'seen,' or 'understood,' what causes 'stumbling' for those who do not know ('understand') it. What Thomas has 'seen' ...his already-attained 'understanding' of 'ⲡⲥⲟⲟⲩⲛⲛ̄ⲧⲙⲏⲉ,' will, therefore, express 'itself in...[his] way of life.'" Perkins' critique of Turner's, and my own, interpretation of 138,16-21 -- if it should be correct -- does nothing to invalidate the points I have demonstrated about the implications of those lines for the formal definition of "ⲡⲥⲟⲟⲩⲛ ⲛ̄ⲧⲙⲏⲉ" as a technical term.

CHAPTER II

1) I have two reasons for restricting my discussion of the "basic teaching" of Thom. Cont. to that found in what Turner has designated "section A." 1) I have already stated the view that it seems rather presumptuous to dismiss casually Turner's quite substantially argued redaction analysis -- at least his basic division of the text into two sources -- as a hypothesis which can safely be ignored in discussing Thom. Cont. 2) Some of the teachings of "section A" suggestive of the thesis I adduce in this study are precisely those which are found throughout the entire tractate. If I were to ig-

nore my own caveat stated just above, I could thus be accused, not only of rejecting Turner's source hypothesis in a rather cavalier fashion, but of doing so because the thesis of this study would be (in some ways at least) more easily demonstrable if the text were taken as an unredacted unity -- or as basically reflecting the point of view of a final redactor seen in both "sections." Therefore, for the purposes of this study, it seems appropriate to restrict the analysis to that of the section -- "section A" -- in which the crucial technical term "ⲡⲥⲟⲟⲩⲛⲛ̄ⲧⲙⲏⲉ" appears.

2) John Douglas Turner, <u>The Book of Thomas the Contender from Codex II of the Cairo Gnostic Library from Nag Hammadi (CG II,7)</u>, 5.
3) CG II: 138,9-10; my translation.
4) CG II: 139,33b-37; Turner's translation, <u>Book of Thomas</u>, 15.
5) CG II: 140,20b-21a, 25, 28b-31a, 32-33; Turner's translation, <u>Book of Thomas</u>, 17, 19.
6) CG II: 139,8-11a; Turner's translation, <u>Book of Thomas</u>, 13.
7) CG II: 139,2b-8a; Turner's translation, <u>Book of Thomas</u>, 13.
8) CG II: 139,25-26a, 27b-29; again Turner's translation, <u>Book of Thomas</u>, 15; emphasis added.
9) CG II: 140,1-4a; Turner's translation, <u>Book of Thomas</u>, 17; emphasis added.
10) Turner points out ("New Link," 112.) that the specific theme of "bestiality" and the use of the technical term "ⲉⲡⲓⲑⲩⲙⲓⲁ" ("$\epsilon\pi\iota\vartheta\nu\mu\iota\alpha$") are limited to "section A." (It is, as I have already suggested, this sort of phenomenon which makes the <u>basic</u> division of the text into the two sources, for which Turner argues, not easily dismissed.) I should point out, nevertheless, that the same basically <u>ascetic point of view</u> (especially defined in terms of anti-sexual asceticism) pervades "section B" also -- even though the "bestiality" motif and the technical term "ⲉⲡⲓⲑⲩⲙⲓⲁ" used to express it are to be found only in "section A."
11) In Foerster, <u>Coptic Sources</u>, 110.
12) <u>Book of Thomas</u>, 120. Turner's use of the phrase "recondite or advanced knowledge" must represent quotation of Lampe's definition of "$\beta\acute{\alpha}\vartheta o\varsigma$" (G.W.H. Lampe, ed., <u>A Patristic Greek Lexicon</u>, 282). I should note -- in light of the discussion in a subsequent chapter -- that Lampe cites Hippolytus's use of that Greek term to describe the specific type of speculation in which "Gnostics" indulged.
13) My translation; emphasis added. In light of this language, and Turner's statement just quoted, I find another statement by Turner which, certainly <u>appears</u> merely to <u>equate</u> "self-knowledge" with this "knowledge of the Depth ($\beta\acute{\alpha}\vartheta o\varsigma$) of the All," rather puzzling. "In section A the Savior functions as revealer, who must get the recipient of the revelation to know himself, his true estate, and thus his destiny: 'the one who knew [sic] himself has already obtained knowledge of the depth [sic] of the All' (138:17f) [sic] " (<u>Book of Thomas</u>, 229).
14) <u>Coptic Sources</u>, 110.

15) CG II: 139,28-29; Turner's translation, Book of Thomas, 15. "ⲥⲱⲧⲡ̄," "chosen, elect person or thing" (W.E. Crum, comp., A Coptic Dictionary, 365), translates the Greek "ἐκλεκτός" fifteen times in the Sahidic Coptic New Testament and all other Greek terms (three) only nine times (Michel Wilmet, Concordance du Nouveau Testament Sahidique, vol. 2, Les Mots Autochtones, 843).
16) CG II: 141,19-22a; Turner's translation, Book of Thomas, 21, 23. The usage of "ἤ" may well represent its function: "to introduce a question which is parallel to a preceding one or supplements it" (BGD, 342).
17) CG II: 141,25-27a; Turner's translation, Book of Thomas, 23; emphasis added.
18) Book of Thomas, 129.
19) Ibid., 157.
20) That is, the attempt to "describe" the Supreme Being and his relationship to mankind and the cosmos.
21) It appears as a Christological epithet (probably) fifteen times (e.g.: at 1 Tim. 1:12; 6:3,14). No attempt will be made in this section to cite every usage of a term in the Greek text. The standard concordances may be consulted by the reader. I, of course, have examined every use of each relevant term in the Pastorals.
22) Tit. 2:13 will not be included in this discussion because of the textual variant involved there. The Pastorals' usage of the term "σωτήρ," vis-à-vis the rest of the New Testament, has, of course, been a frequent subject of discussion. See (for example) Martin Dibelius and Hans Conzelmann, The Pastoral Epistles, 143-46.
23) 2 Tim. 1:10; Tit. 1:14; 3:6.
24) Book of Thomas, 231.
25) 1 Tim. 4:10.
26) 1 Tim. 6:16.
27) Tit. 1:2.
28) 1 Tim. 6:16.
29) 1 Tim. 3:16.
30) 1 Tim. 2:5.
31) Book of Thomas, 226; emphasis added to "hierarchy of divine beings or hypostases, at least in section A."
32) Turner's translation, Book of Thomas, 37.
33) Turner, Book of Thomas, 192; emphasis added.
34) Ibid., 225.
35) Ibid., 226. I have also already pointed out the enigmatic and problematic nature of the only possibly directly "theological" statement in the tractate -- in "section B."
36) Ibid., 231.
37) BGD, 616.
38) Howard Clark Kee, Franklin W. Young and Karlfried Froehlich, Understanding the New Testament, 259; emphasis added.
39) Martin Dibelius, "ἐπίγνωσις ἀληθείας," 2. The term appears at: 1 Tim. 1:10; 2 Tim. 4:3; Tit. 1:9; 2:1.
40) Speaking precisely of this Pastoral usage of forms of the verb "ὑγιαίνω" -- literally: "be in good health, be healthy

or <u>sound</u>" -- Bauer suggests: "Thus, in accord w. prevailing usage, Christian teaching is designated as <u>correct</u>...since it is reasonable and appeals to sound intelligence" (<u>BGD</u>, 832).
41) 1 Tim. 4:6-7.
42) 1 Tim. 6:3-4.
43) 1 Tim. 6:20.
44) See note 3 to Chapter I.
45) See Dibelius's excursus on 1 Tim. 1:10 for examples (Martin Dibelius, <u>Die Pastoralbriefe</u>, 2d rev. ed., 14-15). The citation from Bauer in note 40 pointed out, similarly, that this usage of "ὑγιαίνω" was "in accord w. prevailing usage ...."
46) 1 Tim. 4:4a. It will be pointed out below that there is a specifically Christian cultic motif involved in the statements at 1 Tim. 4:3-4, a fact which makes those statements even more strikingly relevant than if they were to be taken as "abstract" declarations about "the nature of things."
47) 1 Tim. 4:3a; emphasis added.
48) 1 Tim. 4:2.
49) 1 Tim. 2:3-4; emphasis added.
50) Tit. 2:11; emphasis added.
51) CG II: 140,1-4a; Turner's translation, <u>Book of Thomas</u>, 17; emphasis added.
52) Turner, <u>Book of Thomas</u>, 147; emphasis added.
53) <u>Ibid.</u>, 232; emphasis added.
54) <u>Ibid.</u>; emphasis added.
55) See the discussion above, based on 1 Tim. 4:2-4. Other passages in the Pastorals could also be cited.
56) 2 Tim. 2:22a.
57) [Werner] Foerster, <u>TDNT</u>, 7:183. Foerster uses the phrase with specific reference to the Greek "εὐσέβεια."
58) Rudolph Bultmann, <u>Theology of the New Testament</u>, 2:184. He also uses the phrase there in a discussion of "εὐσέβεια."
59) These terms are not, of course, a <u>translation</u> of "εὐσέβεια" -- literally: "<u>piety</u>, <u>godliness</u>, <u>religion</u>" (BGD, 326). The words "<u>moderation</u>" and "<u>self-control</u>" refer, naturally, to the basic <u>definition</u> of "σωφροσύνη" (<u>Ibid.</u>, 802).
60) "This is good, and it is acceptable in the sight of God our Savior, who desires all men to be saved and to come to the knowledge of the truth."
61) 1 Tim. 2:1-2; emphasis added.
62) Tit. 2:11-12; emphasis added.
63) 2 Tim. 4:1-2a.
64) 2 Tim. 4:3-4; emphasis added.
65) This is not to deny, of course, that in important ways the emphases placed upon various facets of that "gospel message" in the Pastorals are often quite different from what is to be found in the genuine Pauline epistles. Also, as will be specifically pointed out below, some important elements of the teaching found in the so-called "kerygmatic" passages of the New Testament are almost totally lacking in the Pastorals. Nevertheless, the crucial areas of agreement which

link the Pastorals' basic message to that of the rest of the New Testament, and which are particularly relevant to this study, are -- to say the least -- considerable!
66) 2 Tim. 1:8b-9; emphasis added.
67) Tit. 3:4-7a; emphasis added.
68) 1 Tim. 1:15-16; emphasis added.
69) Book of Thomas, 231; emphasis added.
70) Emphasis added.
71) Emphasis added.
72) BGD, 75.
73) [Friedrich] Büchsel, TDNT, 4:349.
74) Ibid.
75) I owe almost all of the discussion below on the meaning of "ἀντίλυτρον" and "λυτρώσηται" to Büchsel's, in my opinion, brilliantly cogent analysis in TDNT.
76) Büchsel, TDNT, 4:344; emphasis added to "substitute" and to "ransom." The phrase, "price of release," is taken from the definition of "λύτρον" in BGD, 482.
77) See his entire discussion, TDNT, 4:341-49.
78) Ibid., 345; emphasis added.
79) [Albrecht] Oepke, TDNT, 4:607; emphasis added.
80) Turner, Book of Thomas, 231.
81) 2 Tim. 2:8,11.
82) BGD, 317.
83) Emphasis added.
84) BGD, 180; emphasis added to "agency" and "agent."
85) Turner, Book of Thomas, 229; emphasis added.
86) 1 Tim. 2:7a.
87) Emphasis added.
88) 2 Tim. 1:11.
89) 1 Tim. 6:12a; emphasis added.
90) 1 Tim. 6:14-15; emphasis added.
91) Robert A. Spivey and D. Moody Smith, Anatomy of the New Testament, 399; emphasis added to: "in intention is the Savior of all, not a special class"; "no man stands"; "outside the potential realm of God's redemption."
92) 1 Tim. 2:3-4.
93) Tit. 2:11.
94) Kee, Young and Froehlich, Understanding the New Testament, 259.
95) TDNT, 4:349; emphasis added.
96) Ibid.; emphasis added.
97) Spivey and Smith, Anatomy of the New Testament, 399.

CHAPTER III

1) This reconstruction may appear almost self-evident to Coptic specialists. The purpose of this study, however, is to utilize evidence made available by specialized Coptic-Gnostic

studies in order to shed light upon a problem of importance to New Testament scholarship in general. I thus hopefully assume that not all its readers are Coptic specialists. I shall, therefore, outline -- as briefly as possible -- the reasoning and evidence responsible for the reconstruction in question.

2) "ⲙⲏⲉ" represents a well attested Sahidic variant spelling of the noun "ⲙⲉ," "truth, justice" (W.E. Crum, comp., A Coptic Dictionary, 156).

3) Michel Wilmet, Concordance du Nouveau Testament Sahidique, vol. 2, Les Mots Autochtones, 331. In fifty of those sixty-two differing cases the Coptic translates either the adjective "ἀληθής" or the adjective "ἀληθινός." "ἀλήθεια" is also the first Greek word cited by Crum attested as translated by "ⲙⲉ" (Coptic Dictionary, 156).

4) René Draguet, Index Copte et Grec-Copte de la Concordance du Nouveau Testament Sahidique (CSCO 124, 173, 183, 185), 51.

5) The "ⲧ-" of "ⲛ̄ⲧⲙⲏⲉ" is the definite article used with feminine, singular nouns (Walter C. Till, Koptische Grammatik [Saïdischer Dialekt], §87). A nominal form, such as "ⲙⲏⲉ," when used to represent attributive adjective modification ("Das Attribut"), always "folgt artikellos seinem Regens" (Ibid., §114; emphasis added).

6) See note 3 above.

7) Till, Koptische Grammatik, §114.

8) Ibid., §111.

9) See note 5 above.

10) "Knowledge" (Crum, Coptic Dictionary, 370).

11) Wilmet, Concordance, 860.

12) Draguet, Index Copte et Grec-Copte, 71, 93.

13) L.-Th. Lefort, Concordance du Nouveau Testament Sahidique, vol. 1, Les Mots d'Origine Grecque, 57, 102. One is tempted to suggest (speculate) that the possibly "already discredited" -- to the orthodox at least -- character of the word "γνῶσις" (See p. 3 above and note 3 to Chapter I.) might be at least partially responsible for this phenomenon.

14) See below for a sample of the evidence.

15) I have used, as my sources of evidence: all eight tractates from Codex VI, as indexed by Krause and Labib (Gnost. herm. Schriften, 215, 225-26); CG V,2-5, as indexed by Böhlig and Labib (Alexander Böhlig and Pahor Labib, eds. and trans., Koptisch-Gnostische Apokalypsen aus Codex V von Nag Hammadi im Koptischen Museum zu Alt-Kairo, 123, 129-30; CG II,7, as indexed by Turner (Book of Thomas, 51, 61-62) and Krause and Labib (Gnost. herm. Schriften, 215, 225-26); and CG II,3, The Gospel of Philip, as indexed by Till (Walter C. Till, ed. and trans., Das Evangelium nach Philippos, 87, 93) and Ménard (Jacques É. Ménard, L'Évangile selon Philippe, 250, 268).

16) Only a very few Coptic nouns are "inflected" or "declined" -- at least in the sense those terms are used of Greek, etc. Case, gender, and number must, therefore, be indicated by use of the article and other elements -- such as the "ⲛ̄-" of

the "genitive expression." Since none of the elements used to indicate "case" are reflected in the form "ⲡⲥⲟⲟⲩⲛ," that term almost certainly should be taken as translation of a Greek nominative form.
17) "ⲡ-" is the definite article used with singular, masculine nouns (Till, Koptische Grammatik, §87).
18) This assertion represents a phenomenon known to all students of Coptic and need not be documented at length here.
19) Wilmet, Concordance, 861.
20) Till, Koptische Grammatik, §111.
21) Omn. Prob. Lib. 11.74. Abbreviations used for works of antiquity and the early Christian era are either self-explanatory or those used in TDNT. See TDNT, 1:XVI-XL.
22) TDNT, 1:XXII.
23) Diss. 2.20.21.
24) Maximus was an "eclectic Platonist with Cynical and Stoic tendencies" who flourished in the late second century of the Christian era (TDNT, 1:XXVIII).
25) Philosophumena 26.5b.
26) [Rudolf] Bultmann, TDNT, 1:707, note 30.
27) Ref. 10.31. The Greek text cited is found in Paul Jacques Migne, ed., Patrologiae Cursus Completus...Series Graeca... Cursuum Completorum...Ramos Editore, 16:3446C. The English translation of Refutatio Omnium Haeresium used is that found in Alexander Roberts and James Donaldson, eds., The Ante-Nicene Fathers, vol.5, Hippolytus, Cyprian, Caius, Novatian, Appendix, 19-153 (hereafter cited as ANF). In that translation "Book X" is divided differently than in the Greek; the passage in question is found in ANF at 10.27.
28) Johannes Quasten, Patrology, vol.2, The Ante-Nicene Literature after Irenaeus, 167-68; emphasis added to "tenth book," "an exposition of the true doctrine."
29) Roberts and Donaldson, ANF, 139; emphasis added to: "as a crowning stroke"; "concerning the truth, and to furnish our delineation of this in one book, namely the tenth"; "also"; "to know the power of the truth"; "in the way of salvation."
30) Ibid., 150.
31) My translation from Migne's text (Patrologiae, 16:3446C).
32) G.W.H. Lampe, ed., A Patristic Greek Lexicon, 318; emphasis added to "identified with Christian doctrine," "sometimes called."
33) Roberts and Donaldson, ANF, 150.
34) One can only speculate as to whether or not it is a coincidence that Hippolytus used a technical term ("σωφροσύνη") employed by the Pastorals to characterize the "way of life" led by one who has understood "ἐπίγνωσις ἀληθείας" to describe the "way of life" of those who have been "trained" in "ἀληθείας γνώσει."
35) Roberts and Donaldson, ANF, 152.
36) Ibid., 152-53; emphasis added.
37) Admittedly, Hippolytus's basic (technical) term for "correct Christian doctrine" is simply: "the truth." His goal is to proclaim: "THE DOCTRINE OF THE TRUTH" (Ibid., 150). Still,

as Lampe suggests -- and as the immediate context in which "ἀληθείας γνώσει" appears at 10.31 makes clear by itself -- that phrase there does carry the same meaning as the more frequently used term "ἀλήθεια." Although not Hippolytus's basic (technical) term for "correct Christian doctrine," the phrase in question which does represent that "doctrine" in the context of 10.31 -- and probably also represents the two other facets of the formal definition of "ⲡⲥⲟⲟⲩⲛ̄ⲛ̄ⲧⲙⲏⲉ" and "ἐπίγνωσις ἀληθείας" -- must, therefore, be taken seriously in this historical survey.

38) [Gustav] Stählin, TDNT, 9:169; emphasis added.
39) James Hardy Ropes, A Critical and Exegetical Commentary on the Epistle of St. James, 223; emphasis added.
40) Roberts and Donaldson, ANF, 148-50.
41) Ibid., 10; emphasis added.
42) Ibid., 115; emphasis added.
43) Ibid., 112.
44) Ibid., 124.
45) 1 Tim. 5:23.
46) Hermann Gustav Eduard Krüger, "Encratites," The New Schaff-Herzog Encyclopedia of Religious Knowledge, 4:124.
47) Oxford Dictionary of the Christian Church, s.v. "Encratites."
48) Krüger, "Encratites," 124; emphasis added.
49) Norman McLean, "Marcionism," Encyclopaedia of Religion and Ethics, 8:407. His connection of some sort, at some time, with the "Gnostic teacher Cerdo" seems rather well attested (Hermann Gustav Eduard Krüger, "Marcion, Marcionites," New Schaff-Herzog Encyclopedia, 7:172).
50) Roberts and Donaldson, ANF, 110-12.
51) Encyclopaedia Britannica, 12th ed., s.v. "Empedocles." See it and other standard reference works on the quite complex theories of Empedocles.
52) Oxford Dictionary of the Christian Church, s.v. "Marcion."
53) Krüger, "Marcion, Marcionites," 172.
54) Ibid., 173.
55) McLean, "Marcionism," 408; emphasis added.
56) (New) Columbia Encyclopedia, 4th ed., s.v. "Marcion."
57) Krüger, "Marcion, Marcionites," 172.
58) McLean, "Marcionism," 408; emphasis added.
59) Ibid.; emphasis added.
60) Oxford Dictionary of the Christian Church, s.v. "Marcion"; emphasis added.
61) (New) Columbia Encyclopedia, 4th ed., s.v. "Marcion"; emphasis added.
62) It has often been suggested, of course, that the condemnation of "ἀντιθέσεις" at 1 Tim. 6:20 might be a reference to Marcion's Antitheses; and that, therefore, the Pastorals may be specifically "anti-Marcionite." Quite recently, however, Charles M. Nielsen ("Scripture in the Pastoral Epistles," 4-23) has resurrected the view that -- at least with regard to their view of scripture -- the Pastorals may actually represent what might be called (my phrase) a "proto-Marcionite" view. The only place Jesus is related to the Old Testament

in the Pastorals is at 2 Tim. 2:8: "...descended from David ...." The point of possible relevance to this discussion, however, is that the Pastorals' great emphasis upon teaching that the God who is the Father of Jesus Christ "desires all men to be saved" (1 Tim. 2:4) does "sound" greatly like at least that part of Marcion's theology which so greatly emphasized the grace and love of the New Testament God who is the Father of Jesus Christ. While, in any case, I do not really wish to argue that the Pastorals are "Marcionite" in the least, it is certainly clear that the "false teachers" they attack were not "proto-Marcionites" -- except for the fact that they did apparently reflect the same ascetic view of the Christian "way of life" as that taught by Marcion.

63) Krüger, "Marcion, Marcionites," 172; emphasis added.
64) Roberts and Donaldson, ANF, 142; emphasis added to "chosen," "called," and "captive."
65) Ibid., 47; emphasis added. It is quite worthy of note that "the depths" represents "τὰ βάθη" in the Greek text (Migne, Patrologiae, 16:3126A). In the Greek the citation would be Ref. 5.6. This usage of "βάθη" by Hippolytus, designating Gnostic "esoteric speculation," should make it clear -- if there was ever any doubt -- that in Thom. Cont. a knowledge of "the Depth (βάθος) of the All" represents an "esoteric" type of knowledge which is something additional to "self-knowledge." See note 13 to Chapter II, in which I question Turner's language which -- in one case at least -- merely seems to equate this "knowledge of the Depth (βάθος) of the All" with "self-knowledge." The point I presume here, that in "section A" of Thom. Cont. the emphasis upon such "esoteric speculation" is clearly secondary to the emphasis upon the need for "ascetic self-knowledge," nevertheless still seems quite clear.
66) The summary of Basilides's system requires almost two pages in English translation (Roberts and Donaldson, ANF, 144-45), a summary of the system initially described in nine pages (Ibid., 100-108). The doctrine of the "Docetae" requires a similarly lengthy summary (Ibid., 145-46), a summary of an original four-page description (Ibid., 117-20).
67) Otto Zöckler, "Hippolytus," New Schaff-Herzog Encyclopedia, 5:293; emphasis added.
68) Roberts and Donaldson, ANF, 80; emphasis added.
69) See p. 10 above.
70) See my argument on pp. 38-41 above showing that neither the "Encratites" nor the "Marcionites" can be -- in any conceivable fashion -- equated with those represented by the "basic teaching" of "section A" of Thom. Cont.
71) Haer. 4.33.8.
72) See p. 32 above and note 5 to this chapter.

CHAPTER IV

1) The Gospel of Philip (hereafter cited in notes and text as Gos. Phil.) is found at CG II: 51,29-86,19. The relevant portion of logion 110 consists of CG II: 77,15-30a. There is a vast secondary literature on Gos. Phil., which was one of the first Nag Hammadi texts to be published and attract attention. For full citation of that literature, see David M. Scholer, Nag Hammadi Bibliography 1948-1969, 165-71, and Scholer's supplements to that bibliography which appear almost annually in the fall issue of Novum Testamentum. The basic works which will be taken into account here include the most recent translation of the text, accompanied by a brief but useful introduction (Wesley W. Isenberg, NH. in English, 131-51), and three older "standard" translations with extended commentary. Two of those three works, already cited in another context, also contain the translator's establishment of the Coptic text (Till, Das Evangelium nach Philippos; Ménard, L'Evangile selon Philippe). The third older "standard" work to which I shall refer is that of R. McL. Wilson, The Gospel of Philip. Martin Krause has published a German translation of Gos. Phil., accompanied by a brief introduction, which is also available now in English translation (Coptic Sources, 76-101). His very brief introductory remarks on the tractate have been taken into account in the analysis of Gos. Phil. in this chapter. For purposes of my own study I have, of course, transcribed the relevant portion of the text from the facsimile edition (The Facsimile Edition of the Nag Hammadi Codices: Codex II, 89).
2) CG II: 77,16.
3) CG II: 77,23.
4) CG II: 77,15b-18. All translation of the relevant part of this logion is mine, based upon my transcription of the text from the facsimile edition.
5) Gos. Phil. has even been called an "apocryphal gospel." It is, in fact, almost self-evident that Gos. Phil. is indeed a "Christian-Gnostic" work. The frequency with which it echoes the canonical New Testament is quite remarkable. Most commentators on the text have considered it as basically a representative of "Valentinian" Gnosticism. "It can be located with confidence as a work deriving from the Valentinian school" (Wilson, Gospel of Philip, 15). Ménard's entire discussion of the text's "Théologie spéculative" (L'Évangile selon Philippe, 10-25) is largely concerned with themes he considers "valentinien." He also suggests, in his treatment of its "Théologie sacramentaire" (Ibid., 25-29), that: "Nous posséderions maintenant certaines précisions sur le sacramentalisme valentinien" (Ibid., 25-26; emphasis added). While the two works just cited represent rather early stages of the research on Gos. Phil., their view on this aspect of its character -- "Valentinian" -- still seems to represent

the consensus. Krause (The English of his remarks on Gos. Phil. in Coptic Sources was translated from the German text of 1971.) states: "The doctrine of...Philip shows affinities with Valentinian teaching....Certainly Valentinian is the sacrament of the bridal chamber as attested in the Gospel of Philip" (Coptic Sources, 77). Isenberg, in his quite recent introduction to Gos. Phil., states that the text is: "Generally Valentinian in character" (NH. in English, 131). I have pointed out this consensus on the tractate's basically "Valentinian" character because even George W. MacRae, who has stressed the "secondary" character of "Christian Gnosticism" ("Nag Hammadi and the New Testament," 147), concedes that: "By the time one gets to Valentinianism, for example, the christianizing process is no longer superficial and we are dealing with an authentic Christian Gnosticism" (Ibid., 149; emphasis added). I can, therefore, see no legitimate reason to question the application of the term "Christian-Gnostic" to Gos. Phil.

6) For example, it is stated: "Some said, 'Mary conceived by the Holy Spirit.' They are in error....When did a woman... conceive by a woman?" (CG II: 55,23-27; Isenberg's translation, NH. in English, 134.)

7) It has already been pointed out that John 8:32-34 is echoed in this particular logion. Even the most cursory reading of any English translation of Gos. Phil. reveals many obvious Johannine echoes. Ménard may be quoted on this point. He notes "qu'il [the writer of Gos. Phil.] est influencé par les auteurs çanoniques du N.T., surtout par S. Jean et par S. Paul" (L'Evangile selon Philippe, 32). It is a matter of special relevance to this study that in this logion, and elsewhere in Gos. Phil., "truth" ("ⲙⲉ" or "ⲁⲗⲏⲑⲉⲓⲁ") often is used in a way which quite clearly seems to reflect the Johannine use of "ἀλήθεια" as a technical term. I cite just one -- quite striking -- example in logion 123. "For truth is like ignorance: while it is hidden it rests in itself, but when it is revealed...it is praised inasmuch as it is stronger than ignorance and error. It gives freedom. The word said, 'If you know the truth, the truth will make you free' (John 8:32)....Knowledge is freedom. If we know the truth, we shall find the fruits of the truth within us" (CG II: 84,2-13a; Isenberg's translation, NH. in English, 150).

8) See, for example: John 14:16-17,26; 15:26; 16:13.

9) CG II: 52,21b-24; Isenberg's translation, NH. in English, 132.

10) This is an obvious echo of 1 Cor. 8:1b, as most of the secondary literature points out.

11) All text editions and translations I have seen reconstruct the text as I have.

12) Admittedly, the "freedom" associating men with the slavery to "love" here is directly linked only with "ⲅⲛⲱⲥⲓⲥ" -- not "the knowledge of the truth." It seems, though, in light of the context already noted which (at CG II: 77,23-24) does there associate "freedom" with "the knowledge (γνῶσις) of

the truth (ἀλήθεια)" -- "ⲧⲅⲛⲱⲥⲓⲥⲛ̄ⲧⲁⲗⲏⲑⲉⲓⲁ" -- that in these final statements about the "free one," the one spoken of as "free (ἐλεύθερος) by knowledge (γνῶσις)" (77,26b-27a), probably represents one having the same freedom gained by "the knowledge (γνῶσις) of the truth (ἀλήθεια)" -- a freedom also directly associated with "the knowledge of the truth" at 77, 16 -- "the knowledge of the truth" as "ⲧⲅⲛⲱⲥⲓⲥⲛ̄ⲧⲙⲉ."

13) Even if (See note 12 above.) slavery to "love" is directly associated here only with "ⲅⲛⲱⲥⲓⲥ," and not with "the knowledge (γνῶσις) of the truth (ἀλήθεια)," it is clear that "not sinning" ("It is not given to them to sin....") again, just in itself, associates a "way of life" with "the knowledge of the truth" in this section -- as well as at CG II: 77,15-18.
14) The phrases are translated in such a literal way by Wilson (<u>Gospel of Philip</u>, 53).
15) Ménard translates (at both 77,20 and 77,22) : "Ceux à qui il n'est pas permis de pécher" (<u>L'Évangile selon Philippe</u>, 99). Till translates the phrases (again identically) : "denen es sich erlaubt ist zu sündigen" (<u>Evangelium nach Philippos</u>, 55).
16) Crum, <u>Coptic Dictionary</u>, 392-93.
17) BGD, 262.
18) Crum, <u>Coptic Dictionary</u>, 790; Wilmet, <u>Concordance</u>, 1666-67. I have studied the examples cited by Crum and Wilmet and can not, frankly, understand Ménard's remark: "Le verbe copte ϫⲓⲥⲉ ⲛ̄ϩⲏⲧ...n'a jamais un sens péjorative en saïdique" (<u>L'Évangile selon Philippe</u>, 227).
19) See note 12 above.
20) When, for example, one compares Wilson's translation of the section in question with Isenberg's, it really does almost seem that he is reading translations of two different Coptic texts.
21) See, again, note 12 above.
22) "The one who has become free (ἐλεύθερος) through knowledge (γνῶσις) is a slave...for those...not yet...able to receive [the fr]eedom ([ἐ]λευθερία) of the knowledge (γνῶσις)."
23) Also see p. 46 above where it was pointed out that the Gnostic commonplace representing "ⲅⲛⲱⲥⲓⲥ" as the ultimate Revelation may be seen reflected elsewhere in <u>Gos. Phil.</u> -- and expressed by statements about "the Father" at 52,21-24 and in this logion.
24) It should also be pointed out that the "intent" of a writer such as T.S. Eliot seems not to have been influenced by the fact that he could hardly have expected "most" readers to "understand" his poetry.
25) For the purposes of this survey, unless indicated otherwise, I quote from Isenberg's translation of <u>Gos. Phil.</u> in <u>NH. in English</u>, giving the page number there and also designating what lines of CG II are translated by the English quoted.
26) <u>NH. in English</u>, 139 (66,4b-6).
27) <u>NH. in English</u>, 139 (65,27-30a).
28) <u>NH. in English</u>, 132 (52,35b-53,9); emphasis added.
29) <u>NH. in English</u>, 140 (67,24).

30) NH. in English, 136 (59,11b-12).
31) NH. in English, 137 (61,36-62,5); emphasis added.
32) I have also already pointed out the possible significance of the teaching about a slavery to "love" in logion 110 -- a "love" for those who would, in fact, be considered "blind men" to be "despised" in Thom. Cont.
33) NH. in English, 135 (59,2b-6a); emphasis added.
34) I certainly do not mean to deny that there is, as I pointed out initially in this comparison, much ascetic and "anti-worldly" teaching in Gos. Phil. Gos. Phil., however, does not define its version of "Christianity" almost exclusively -- as does Thom. Cont. -- in terms of an obsessive, almost psychotic, anti-sexuality.
35) NH. in English, 143 (72,4b-8); emphasis added.
36) NH. in English, 141 (69,1-4); emphasis added.
37) In note 10 to Chapter II I have already indicated that the actual motif of man's "bestiality" -- as well as the somewhat closely related technical term "ⲉⲡⲓⲑⲩⲙⲓⲁ" -- are only found in "section A" of Thom. Cont., not appearing in "section B." I am, in any case of course, only interested in differentiating the "basic teaching" of Gos. Phil. from that of "section A" of Thom. Cont. It should be evident, however, as pointed out in that previous note, that the radically anti-sexual view of the whole of Thom. Cont. does not depend either upon the technical usage of "ⲉⲡⲓⲑⲩⲙⲓⲁ" or the specific motif of man's "bestiality." In this one particular case -- perhaps -- it is easier to differentiate the "basic teaching" of Gos. Phil. from just that of "section A" than from that of the entirety of Thom. Cont. It should be quite clear, however, from the whole of the present discussion, that the "basic teaching" of Gos. Phil. would still be quite sharply differentiated from that found in "section A" of Thom. Cont. -- even if the latter did not utilize either the motif of "bestiality" or the technical term "ⲉⲡⲓⲑⲩⲙⲓⲁ" to represent its basic view of the (anti-sexual) content of "Christianity."
38) NH. in English, 138-39 (64,12b-22); emphasis added.
39) The Apocalypse of Adam (hereafter cited in text and notes as Apoc. Adam) is found at CG V: 64,1-85,32. The first establishment of the text, accompanied by a German translation and extensive commentary, was that of Böhlig and Labib in Koptisch-Gnostische Apokalypsen aus Codex V, 86-117. More recently, Charles Webster Hedrick has written an extensive study of the tractate which also includes his English translation based upon his establishment of the text. That text (and the translation) are not presented consecutively, however, but in a way meant to reflect the reconstruction of the sources hypothesized in his redaction analysis of the text ("The Apocalypse of Adam"). In most cases his dissertation will be cited according to the pagination of its published form (The Apocalypse of Adam). I shall, however, also quote two statements from the dissertation's abstract, an abstract not contained in the published version. That pub-

lication is, however, only an almost totally verbatim reproduction of the original dissertation. It certainly contains absolutely no change in the content of the dissertation's argument! It, therefore, seems quite legitimate to quote the language of the dissertation's abstract as a fair representation of the content of Hedrick's monograph -- when that language of the abstract is particularly appropriate. George W. MacRae has also published an English translation, along with a brief but useful introduction, in NH. in English, 256-64. He has also presented that translation, accompanied by his establishment of the Coptic text and another introduction, in his "The Apocalypse of Adam." The German translation of Apoc. Adam by Krause, again accompanied by a brief introduction, is also available in English translation in Coptic Sources, 13-23. Again, of course, the purpose of this study is not to present a complete analysis of Apoc. Adam. The reader interested in a more complete and detailed study of that text should consult: Scholer's Nag Hammadi Bibliography, 182; Scholer's annual bibliographic supplements in Novum Testamentum; Hedrick's Apocalypse of Adam, 9-17 ("History of Research"); and Hedrick's bibliography in Apocalypse of Adam, 299-308.

40) The translation is mine, based upon my transcription of the relevant portion of the text from the facsimile edition (The Facsimile Edition of the Nag Hammadi Codices: Codex V, 93. Neither my transcription or translation differs in any significant way from those of Böhlig-Labib, Hedrick, or MacRae.
41) NH. in English, 256.
42) George W. MacRae, "The Coptic Gnostic Apocalypse of Adam," 28.
43) Ibid., 32.
44) NH. in English, 256.
45) George W. MacRae, "Nag Hammadi and the New Testament," 149.
46) "Coptic Gnostic Apocalypse of Adam," 28; "Nag Hammadi and the New Testament," 149.
47) "Nag Hammadi and the New Testament," 149.
48) NH. in English, 256.
49) George W. MacRae, "The Apocalypse of Adam," 152; emphasis added.
50) "Nag Hammadi and the New Testament," 148; emphasis added.
51) Ibid., 149; emphasis added.
52) Ibid., 153-55.
53) Ibid., 154.
54) Ibid., 155; emphasis added.
55) "Apocalypse of Adam," 152.
56) Ibid.; emphasis added.
57) Koptisch-Gnostische Apokalypsen aus Codex V, 95.
58) Ibid., 90, 93, 95.
59) As a "Visiting Examiner" MacRae signed Hedrick's dissertation, affirming it to be: "adequate in scope and quality" ("Apocalypse of Adam," [v]). On the other hand, it would appear that Krause would not find any such redaction analysis acceptable. "A distribution of the various ideas men-

tioned over individual sources which have been combined together in this document is, however, not in my opinion possible" (<u>Coptic Sources</u>, 15). Those words were, of course, written some years before Hedrick's work was available.
60) "Apocalypse of Adam," [iii]. This statement is, therefore, one of those taken from the dissertation's abstract which does not appear in Hedrick's published monograph.
61) Hedrick, <u>Apocalypse of Adam</u>, 85-87.
62) <u>Ibid</u>., 86.
63) <u>Ibid</u>., 87.
64) <u>Ibid</u>., 240-41.
65) Hedrick, "Apocalypse of Adam," [iii]; emphasis added.
66) Hedrick, <u>Apocalypse of Adam</u>, 97-163.
67) <u>Ibid</u>., 97; emphasis added.
68) <u>Ibid</u>.
69) <u>Ibid</u>., 97-115.
70) <u>Ibid</u>., 109.
71) <u>Ibid</u>., 115.
72) <u>Ibid</u>., 154.
73) <u>Ibid</u>.
74) <u>Ibid</u>., 154-60.
75) <u>Ibid</u>., 159-60; emphasis added.
76) <u>Ibid</u>., 214; emphasis added to "<u>evident lack of Christian influence on the</u>," "<u>in a time before the Sethian movement was Christianized</u>."
77) Krause would appear to be in complete agreement. "Christian material is not present, or at least is not mentioned openly and without disguise. We are...<u>justified in describing this document as...non-Christian gnostic</u>" (<u>Coptic Sources</u>, 15; emphasis added).
78) The only other (technical) usage of "the knowledge of the truth" which that survey has shown to be even possibly relevant to this study is Hippolytus's use of "ἀληθείας γνώσει" in his anti-Gnostic polemic at <u>Ref</u>. 10.31.

CHAPTER V

1) 1 Tim. 2:15a; 5:14a; emphasis added.
2) 1 Tim. 4:4. This "general" statement about the "goodness" of the created world, and also the statement at 1 Tim. 4:3 concerning "abstinence from foods," are not simply abstract declarations of fact. A "[Christian] kultisches Motif" is also involved (Martin Dibelius, <u>Die Pastoralbriefe</u>, 2d rev. ed., 40). "Foods" (1 Tim. 4:3) and "everything created by God" (1 Tim. 4:4) are both to be received "μετὰ εὐχαριστίας" ("with thanksgiving"). It is thus affirmed that God's created things (his entire creation) should be accepted as being "good" especially when received "with thanksgiving" -- that is, by <u>Christians who perceive the nature of the cre-</u>

ator and his created things, and who are "thankful." One might take "εὐχαριστίας" -- in light of Dibelius's use of the phrase "kultisches Motif" -- as possibly representing "sacramental" terminology. It is clear, however, from the context of Dibelius's entire discussion, that he really did intend to indicate the attitude of worshipful "thanksgiving" for the goodness of God and of his creation to which I have just referred. Such Christians, in a certain sense, stand in a "peculiar relationship" (my phrase) to these gifts of the creator. It is said, of the acceptance of "foods" at 1 Tim. 4:3, that they are to be received "with thanksgiving" by "τοῖς πιστοῖς καὶ ἐπεγνωκόσι τὴν ἀλήθειαν" -- "Selbstbezeichnung der Christen" (Dibelius, Pastoralbriefe, 2d rev. ed., 40). They "accept food with thanksgiving and thereby make it holy" (Martin Dibelius and Hans Conzelmann, The Pastoral Epistles, 64). These two "anti-ascetic" statements at 1 Tim. 4:3-4, apparently set in a context specifically affirming that Christians repudiate such asceticism, are thus even more directly relevant -- as statements rejecting such asceticism as an appropriate part of "Christsein" -- than if they were merely "abstract" statements.
3) 1 Tim. 4:3-4 has now been cited three times as directly contradicting parts of the "basic teaching" of "section A" of Thom. Cont. Dibelius suggested, significantly: "IV 1-10 ist der einzige Abschnitt des Briefes, der sich planmässig mit der Irrlehre beshäftigt" (Pastoralbriefe, 2d rev. ed., 40).
4) The context of this particular passage might well indicate that the specific polemic, in this case, is directed against Jews or "Judaizers" who opposed rejection of the Jewish dietary law. At Tit. 1:10 "the circumcision party" is singled out for attack; "Jewish myths" are deprecated at Tit. 1:14. The reference to "commands of men" immediately preceding the statement that "all things" are "pure" could, therefore, be quite logically taken as a reference to that Jewish dietary law. The Pastorals' argument against food-related asceticism, and their argument against excessive "speculation" to be discussed below, both seem partially carried out in an apparently anti-Jewish or "anti-Judaizing" context. Since Thom. Cont. contains no (at least obviously) "Jewish" doctrine, that aspect of the Pastorals' polemic might, therefore, seem to present a problem for the thesis I intend to propose. I shall explain below, however -- in some detail -- why I believe this aspect of the Pastorals' polemic does not really affect the basic relationship I find between the ideology of "section A" of Thom. Cont. and the false teachings attacked by the Pastorals.
5) "This is good and it is acceptable in the sight of God our Savior, who desires all men to be saved and to come to the knowledge of the truth. For there is one God, and there is one mediator between God and men, the man Christ Jesus, who gave himself as a ransom for all...."
6) See p. 29 above.
7) See note 3 above.

8) <u>Pastoralbriefe</u>, 2d rev. ed., 41.
9) See note 4 above.
10) This fourth aspect of the false teachings I find represented in "section A" of <u>Thom. Cont.</u> is thus also attacked in the most important, in Dibelius's view, passage against false teaching in the Pastorals (1 Tim. 4:1-10). Again, see note 3 above.
11) Dibelius and Conzelmann, <u>The Pastoral Epistles</u>, 17; emphasis added. This statement is not found in the 2d rev. German ed. of 1931. It first appears in the 3d German ed. (1955) revised by Conzelmann; and reflects research unavailable to Dibelius himself (Martin Dibelius, <u>Die Pastoralbriefe</u>, 3d ed., 15; Dibelius and Conzelmann, <u>The Pastoral Epistles</u>, 17, note 16).
12) The quotation in question is, admittedly, taken out of context when applied to <u>Thom. Cont.</u> It is meant to describe the false teachers as representatives of "early Jewish or Judaizing forms of Gnosticism" (Dibelius and Conzelmann, <u>The Pastoral Epistles</u>, 17). The <u>actual language</u>, however, so <u>perfectly describes</u> the key elements of the "basic teaching" of "section A" of <u>Thom. Cont.</u>!
13) <u>Pastoralbriefe</u>, 2d rev. ed., 41-43. The summary is basically unchanged in Dibelius and Conzelmann, <u>The Pastoral Epistles</u>, 65-67.
14) <u>Apol.</u> 1.26.4.
15) <u>Haer.</u> 1.23.5.
16) It is clearly enunciated in, for example, <u>The Treatise on Resurrection</u> (CG I,4) and <u>Gos. Phil.</u>
17) Dibelius also characterizes the "Irrlehrer" in the Pastorals by use of the term "Enthusiasmus" (<u>Pastoralbriefe</u>, 2d rev. ed., 41) -- "Enthusiasm" (Dibelius and Conzelmann, <u>The Pastoral Epistles</u>, 65). It seems almost certain, however (at least to me), that those terms really <u>basically</u> refer to what I have been calling "speculation," or the seeking of "esoteric knowledge," etc.
18) See pp. 66-67 above.
19) I have already alluded to this possibility in note 4.
20) The phrase at Tit. 1:10, "οἱ ἐκ τῆς περιτομῆς," is cited by Bauer as an expression which "= the <u>Jewish Christians</u>" (<u>BGD</u>, 653).
21) "For everything created by God is good, and nothing is to be rejected...." The specific context of this statement was, of course, discussed in note 2. I can see no reason to read into it anything affirming a "Christian" view of receiving God's "good" (foods) which is <u>being specifically contrasted</u> with <u>Jewish</u> dietary restrictions. The statement is clearly to be viewed in the context of the more general attack upon asceticism -- food <u>and marriage</u> rejecting -- in the previous verse, an attack which certainly can not specifically refer to Jewish legalism. Dibelius even suggests that the language of this section may, in fact, actually reflect Christian usage influenced by: "die Kultsprache des Judentums" (<u>Pastoralbriefe</u>, 2d rev. ed., 41).

22) Emphasis added. See note 20 on Bauer's interpretation of "οἱ ἐκ τῆς περιτομῆς" in this passage.
23) Pastoralbriefe, 2d rev. ed., 87; emphasis added. The same interpretation is retained in Dibelius and Conzelmann, The Pastoral Epistles, 137. The linking of the use of "μῦθος" at Tit. 1:14 to its usage at 1 Tim. 1:4 is especially significant since Dibelius, apparently, considered that term's meaning at 1 Tim. 1:4 to be quite unspecific: "μῦθος wird hier wohl wie sonst oft zur Kennzeichnung falsher und törichter Erzählungen verwendet" (Pastoralbriefe, 2d rev. ed., 10).
24) Pastoralbriefe, 2d rev. ed., 42.
25) If the Pastorals might conceivably represent even a "semi-proto-Marcionite" view (See note 62 to Chapter III.), such an exaggeration would be even more likely.
26) "Nag Hammadi and the New Testament," 150; emphasis added.
27) Ibid.; emphasis added.
28) Ibid., 149.
29) For example, at 1 Cor. 2:6-8 Paul may have applied a Gnostic theme -- "the deception of the powers" -- to "the passion and death of Jesus" (Ibid., 155).
30) Ibid., 150.
31) See pp. 73-77.

CHAPTER VI

1) As I have already pointed out, the only possible parallel of relevance, which will be taken into account in the discussion below, was found in Hippolytus's anti-Gnostic polemic at Ref. 10.31.
2) I have previously pointed out, for example, that there is no doctrine of a "realized resurrection" -- as that described at 2 Tim. 2:18 -- to be found anywhere in Thom. Cont. (See p. 72.)
Both here and elsewhere I have used the phrase: "the ideology of the group responsible for 'section A' of Thom. Cont." By those statements I simply mean that I take it for granted that some sort of "community-based thought" was the source of the ideology in that "section." I do not mean that the ideology in question necessarily arose from some sort of an ascetic-gnostic "congregation" or group of "congregations." It is, of course, quite possible, however, that the essence of that ideology -- minus the stylistic peculiarities of the actual writer(s) of the text of "section A" and any possible later redactional changes found in the present text -- could have emerged from some rather concrete (or even organized) group.

BIBLIOGRAPHY

Altaner, Berthold. Patrology. Translated by Hilda Graef. Freiburg: Herder and Herder, 1960.
Barrett, Charles Kingsley. The Pastoral Epistles in the New English Bible. The New Clarendon Bible. New Testament, vol. 8. Oxford: Clarendon Press, 1963.
Bauer, Walter. A Greek-English Lexicon of the New Testament and Other Early Christian Literature. Translated by William F. Arndt and F. Wilbur Gingrich. 2d ed., revised by F. Wilbur Gingrich and Frederick W. Danker. Chicago and London: University of Chicago Press, 1979.
Böhlig, Alexander, and Labib, Pahor, eds. and trans. Koptisch-Gnostische Apokalypsen aus Codex V von Nag Hammadi im Koptischen Museum zu Alt-Kairo. Wissenschaftliche Zeitschrift der Martin-Luther-Universität Halle-Wittenberg, Sonderband. Halle-Wittenberg: Martin-Luther-Universität, 1963.
Bultmann, Rudolf. Theology of the New Testament. Translated by Kendrick Grobel. 2 vols. New York: Charles Scribner's Sons, 1951-55.
Cross, F. L., ed. The Oxford Dictionary of the Christian Church. London and New York: Oxford University Press, 1957.
Crum, W. E., comp. A Coptic Dictionary. 1939. Reprint. Oxford: Clarendon Press, 1962.
Dibelius, Martin. "ἐπίγνωσις ἀληθείας." 1914. Reprinted in Botschaft und Geschichte: Gesammelte Aufsätze von Martin Dibelius, edited by Gunther Bornkamm, 2: 1-13. Tübingen: Mohr, 1956.
_____. Die Pastoralbriefe. 2d ed., rev. Handbuch zum Neuen Testament, vol. 13. Tübingen: Mohr, 1931.
_____. Die Pastoralbriefe. 3d ed., revised by Hans Conzelmann. Handbuch zum Neuen Testament, vol. 13. Tübingen: Mohr, 1955.
_____. Die Pastoralbriefe. 4th ed., revised by Hans Conzelmann. Handbuch zum Neuen Testament, vol. 13. Tübingen: Mohr, 1966.
_____, and Conzelmann, Hans. The Pastoral Epistles: A Commentary on the Pastoral Epistles. Translated by Philip Buttolph and Adela Yarbro. Edited by Helmut Koester. Philadelphia: Fortress Press, 1972.
Dornier, Pierre. Les Épitres Pastorales. Paris: J. Gabalda,1969.
Draguet, René. Index Copte et Grec-Copte de la Concordance du Nouveau Testament Sahidique (CSCO 124, 173, 183, 185). Corpus Scriptorum Christianorum Orientalium, vol. 196. Louvain: Secrétariat du CorpusSCO, 1960.
Easton, Burton Scott. The Pastoral Epistles; An Introduction, Translation, Commentary and Word Studies. New York: Charles Scribner's Sons, 1947.
The Facsimile Edition of the Nag Hammadi Codices: Codex II. Leiden: Brill, 1974.
The Facsimile Edition of the Nag Hammadi Codices: Codex V. Leiden: Brill, 1975.

Foerster, Werner, comp. Gnosis; a Selection of Gnostic Texts. Vol. 2, Coptic and Mandic Sources. Translated and edited by R. McL. Wilson. Oxford: Clarendon Press, 1974.

Hanson, Anthony Tyrrell. The Pastoral Letters: Commentary on the First and Second Letters to Timothy and the Letter to Titus. Cambridge: Cambridge University Press, 1966.

Hastings, James, ed. Encyclopaedia of Religion and Ethics. 12 vols. Edinburgh: T. & T. Clark, 1908-21.

Hedrick, Charles Webster. "The Apocalypse of Adam: a Literary and Source Analysis." Ph.D. dissertation, Claremont Graduate School, 1977.

_____. The Apocalypse of Adam: a Literary and Source Analysis. Society of Biblical Literature Dissertation Series, vol. 46. Chico, Cal.: Scholars Press, 1980.

Holtz, Gottfried. Die Pastoralbriefe. Theologischer Handkommentar zum Neuen Testament, vol. 13. Berlin: Evangelische Verlagsanstalt, 1965.

Jackson, Samuel MaCauley, ed. The New Schaff-Herzog Encyclopedia of Religious Knowledge. 12 vols. New York: Funk and Wagnalls, 1908-12.

Jeremias, Joachim, and Strathmann, Hermann. Die Briefe an Timotheus und Titus. Der Brief an die Hebräer. 11th ed. Das Neue Testament Deutsch, vol. 9. Göttingen: Vandenhoeck & Ruprecht, 1975.

Kee, Howard Clark; Young, Franklin W.; and Froehlich, Karlfried. Understanding the New Testament. 3d ed. Englewood Cliffs, N.J.: Prentice-Hall, 1973.

Kelly, J. N. D. A Commentary on the Pastoral Epistles; I Timothy, II Timothy, Titus. New York: Harper & Row, 1963.

Kircher, Dankwart. "'Das Buch des Thomas': Die siebte Schrift aus Nag-Hammadi-Codex II." Theologische Literaturzeitung 102 (1977): 793-804.

Kittel, Gerhard, ed. Theological Dictionary of the New Testament. Translated and edited by Geoffrey W. Bromiley. 10 vols. Grand Rapids, Mich.: Eerdmans, 1964-76.

Krause, Martin, and Labib, Pahor. Gnostische und hermetische Schriften aus Codex II und Codex VI. Abhandlungen des Deutschen Archäologischen Instituts Kairo. Koptische Reihe, vol. 2. Glückstadt: Augustin, 1971.

Kümmel, Werner George. Introduction to the New Testament. rev. ed. Translated by Howard Clark Kee. Nashville and New York: Abingdon Press, 1975.

Lampe, G. W. H., ed. A Patristic Greek Lexicon. Oxford: Clarendon Press, 1961.

Lefort, L.-Th. Concordance du Nouveau Testament Sahidique. Vol. 1, Les Mots d'Origine Grecque. Corpus Scriptorum Christianorum Orientalium, vol. 124. Louvain: Imprimerie Orientaliste L. Durbecq, 1950.

Lock, Walter. A Critical and Exegetical Commentary on the Pastoral Epistles (I & II Timothy and Titus). The International Critical Commentary on the Holy Scriptures of the Old and New Testaments, vol. 39. Edinburgh: T. & T. Clark, 1924.

MacRae, George W. "The Coptic Gnostic Apocalypse of Adam." <u>Heythrop Journal</u> 6 (1965): 27-35.
_____. "Nag Hammadi and the New Testament." In <u>Gnosis:Festschrift für Hans Jonas</u>, edited by Barbara Aland, 144-57. Göttingen: Vandenhoeck & Ruprecht, 1978.
_____. "The Apocalypse of Adam." In <u>Nag Hammadi Codices V, 2-5 and VI with Papyrus Berolinensis 8502,1 and 4</u>, edited by D. M. Parrott, 151-95. Leiden: Brill, 1979.
Ménard, Jacques É. <u>L'Évangile selon Philippe: Introduction Texte -Traduction Commentaire</u>. Paris: Letouzey & Ané, 1967.
Migne, Jacques Paul, ed. <u>Patrologiae Cursus Completus...Series Graeca...Cursuum Completorum in Singulos Scientiae Ecclesiasticae Ramos Editore</u>. 161 vols. Paris: Migne, 1857-66.
<u>The Nag Hammadi Library in English: Translated by Members of the Coptic Gnostic Library Project of the Institute for Antiquity and Christianity</u>. San Francisco: Harper & Row, 1977.
Nielsen, Charles M. "Scripture in the Pastoral Epistles." <u>Perspectives in Religious Studies</u> 7 (1980): 4-23.
Quasten, Johannes. <u>Patrology</u>. Vol.2, <u>The Ante-Nicene Literature after Irenaeus</u>. Westminster, Md.: Newman Press, 1953.
Roberts, Alexander, and Donaldson, James, eds. <u>The Ante-Nicene Fathers: Translations of the Writings of the Fathers down to A.D. 325</u>. Vol.5, <u>Hippolytus, Cyprian, Caius, Novatian, Appendix</u>. New York: Charles Scribner's Sons, 1899.
Ropes, James Hardy. <u>A Critical and Exegetical Commentary on the Epistle of St. James</u>. The International Critical Commentary on the Holy Scriptures of the Old and New Testaments, vol. 16. Edinburgh: T. & T. Clark, 1916.
Schlatter, Adolf. <u>Die Kirche der Griechen im Urteil des Paulus: Eine Auslegung seiner Briefe an Timotheus und Titus</u>. 2d ed. Stuttgart: Calwer Verlag, 1958.
Scholer, David M. <u>Nag Hammadi Bibliography 1948-1969</u>. Nag Hammadi Studies, vol. 1 Leiden: Brill, 1971.
Scott, Ernest Findlay. <u>The Pastoral Epistles</u>. The Moffatt New Testament Commentary, vol. 13. London and New York: Harper & Brothers, 1936.
Simpson, E. K. <u>The Pastoral Epistles; the Greek Text with Introduction and Commentary</u>. Grand Rapids, Mich.: Eerdmans, 1954.
Spicq, Ceslaus. <u>Saint Paul; Les Épitres Pastorales</u>. 2 vols. 4th ed., rev. Paris: J. Gabalda, 1969.
Spivey, Robert A., and Smith, D. Moody. <u>Anatomy of the New Testament: A Guide to its Structure and Meaning</u>. 2d ed. New York and London: MacMillan, 1974.
Steindorff, Georg. <u>Lehrbuch der koptischen Grammatik</u>. Chicago: University of Chicago Press, 1951.
Till, Walter C. <u>Koptische Grammatik (Saïdischer Dialekt): mit Bibliographie, Lesestücken und Wörterverzeichnissen</u>. 2d ed., rev. Lehrbücher für das Studium der orientalischen und afrikanischen Sprachen, vol. 1. Leipzig: Veb Verlag Enzyklopädie, 1970.
_____, ed. and trans. <u>Das Evangelium nach Philippos</u>. Patristische Texte und Studien, vol. 2. Berlin: Walter de Gruyter, 1963.

Turner, John Douglas. "A New Link in the Syrian Judas Thomas Tradition." In Essays on the Nag Hammadi Texts in Honour of Alexander Böhlig, edited by Martin Krause. Nag Hammadi Studies, vol. 3, 109-19. Leiden: Brill, 1972.

———. The Book of Thomas the Contender from Codex II of the Cairo Gnostic Library from Nag Hammadi (CG II,7): The Coptic Text with Translation Introduction and Commentary. Society of Biblical Literature Dissertation Series, vol. 23. Missoula, Mont.: Scholars Press, 1975.

Weiss, Bernhard. Die Briefe an Timotheus und Titus. 7th ed., rev. Kritisch exegetisches Kommentar über das Neue Testament, vol. 11. Göttingen: Vandenhoeck & Ruprecht, 1902.

Wilmet, Michel. Concordance du Nouveau Testament Sahidique. Vol. 2, Les Mots Autochtones. 3 vols. Corpus Scriptorum Christianorum Orientalium, vols. 173, 183, 185. Louvain: Secrétariat du CorpusSCO, 1957-59.

Wilson, R. McL. The Gospel of Philip: Translated from the Coptic Text, with an Introduction and Commentary. New York and Evanston: Harper & Row, 1962.

Grimm, Werner
DIE VERKÜNDIGUNG JESU UND DEUTEROJESAJA
Frankfurt/M., Bern, 1981. 2. überarbeitete Auflage von
«Weil Ich dich liebe». XII, 360 S.
Arbeiten zum Neuen Testament und Judentum. Bd. 1
ISBN 3-8204-5943-X   br. sFr. 56.–

Ausgangspunkt ist eine zufällige Entdeckung: Jes. 43,3f – nicht in erster Linie Jes.53 – ist das alttestamentliche Prophetenwort, auf welches die älteste Deutung des Todes Jesu Bezug nimmt. Von daher muss die Frage des Verhältnisses der Botschaft Jesu zur dtjes. Prophetie neu gestellt werden, vor allem mit Hilfe des sprachlichen Vergleichs. Manche dunklen Jesusworte lassen sich nun erhellen, und die christliche Verkündigung der Liebe Gottes wird präzisiert und in ihrer ursprünglichen Intensität freigelegt. Die zweite, überarbeitete und ergänzte Auflage berücksichtigt Fragen und Ergebnisse der Forschung seit 1976.
Aus dem Inhalt: Feststellung und Bewertung zahlreicher deuterojesajanischer Elemente in Jesusworten – Die Messianität Jesu – Das Lösegeldwort Mk. 10,45 als Antwort auf das Heilsorakel Jes. 43,1-7 – Konsequenzen für die christliche Verkündigung des «stellvertretenden Sterbens» Jesu und der Liebe Gottes.

Lauer, Simon (Hrsg.)
KRITIK UND GEGENKRITIK IN CHRISTENTUM UND JUDENTUM
Bern, Frankfurt/M., Las Vegas, 1981. 223 S.
Judaica et Christiana. Bd. 3
ISBN 3-261-04758-5   br. sFr. 48.–

Dass Judentum und Christentum einander stets kritisiert haben, ist bekannt. Dabei wird aber oft übersehen, dass beide Religionen sehr wohl fähig sind, sich selber kritisch zu betrachten und sich in der Begegnung mit dem andern in Frage stellen zu lassen. In Zeiten religiöser, sozialer und politischer Unrast, in denen es zu Verfolgungen aller Grade kommen kann, ist solche Gegenkritik besonders bedeutsam. Dieser Band versucht darzustellen, wann und wo Kritik und Gegenkritik zu finden sind und in welchen Kontext sie gehören. Neutestamentler, Historiker und Philologen beteiligen sich an dieser Arbeit.
Aus dem Inhalt: Judentum, Antike und Neues Testament – Kirche in Altertum und Mittelalter – Russische und französische Literatur – Neuere Schweizergeschichte.

Verlag Peter Lang · Bern und Frankfurt am Main
Auslieferung: Verlag Peter Lang AG, Jupiterstr. 15, CH-3000 Bern 15
Telefon (0041/31) 32 11 22, Telex verl ch 32 420

Augustin, Matthias (Hrsg.) / Kegler, Jürgen (Hrsg.)
DAS ALTE TESTAMENT ALS GEISTIGE HEIMAT
Festgabe für Hans Walter Wolff zum 70. Geburtstag
Frankfurt/M., Bern, 1981. 135 S.
Europäische Hochschulschriften: Reihe 23, Theologie. Bd. 177
ISBN 3-8204-5726-7 . 31.—

Neben seinen wissenscha... ...entler
Hans Walter Wolff auch ... ...orben.
So werden in dieser Fes... ...en des
theologischen Lehrers d... ...ament
weitergegeben hat, sei es ... ...ür das
künftige Pfarramt.
Aus dem Inhalt: U.a. B... ...misti-
schen Königschroniken ... ...Tadel
Jahwes im Alten Testar... ...eine
menschliche Zukunft im A... ...4-17.

Hahn, Joachim
DAS «GOLDENE
Die Jahwe-Verehrung
Frankfurt/M., Bern, 1981.
Europäische Hochschulsch...
ISBN 3-8204-5872-7   71.—

Von Stierbildern des Volke...   Dtn
9,7ff und 1Kön 12,26ff. Di...   sle-
gungs- und Forschungsgesch...   tio-
nen und Beurteilungen de...   ung
sucht die wichtigsten Interp...   und
die Forschungsgeschichte zu...   zu-
stellen und zu beurteilen.
Aus dem Inhalt: U.a. Zum
Die Stierbilder Jerobeams i...   der
Stierbilder – Geschichte der

Verlag Peter Lang · Bern und Frankfurt am Main
Auslieferung: Verlag Peter Lang AG, Jupiterstr. 15, CH-3000 Bern 15
Telefon (0041/31) 32 11 22, Telex verl ch 32 420